Golf Course of Rhymes

William Innes of the Blackheath Club

Golf Course of Rhymes

Links between Golf and Poetry
Through the Ages

Foreword by Robert Trent Jones, Jr.

'The game you were telling me of the other day,
I wish, sir, its meaning you'd explain—do, pray.
Of some outlandish instruments I've heard you speak,
Such as *drivers, putters, short spoons, irons,* and *cleek*;
Bunkers up or down, *odds*, playing *one off two*;
Niblicks, steimies; enlighten me, good sir, do.'
Thus was I addressed, or perhaps I did but dream.
The answer quick was, 'You mean Golf, of games the
cream.'

BLACKHEATH CLUB *GOLFING LAYS*
(Thomas Marsh, Esq., 1873)

Leon S. White, PhD

Golfiana Press: Lexington, MA
2011

ISBN: 978-0-9832137-0-3

Library of Congress Control Number: 2011922115

Cover Photo: The Machrie #8, Isle of Islay, Scotland © Laurence Casey Lambrecht

Cover Design by Sarah Georgakopoulos

Dedication

To my wife and love of my life, Barbara Ehrlich White—the number one author and historian in our family—for her unfailing love, support and encouragement. I can't thank her enough for rooting me on and on and on. And to our sons, Joel and David, who encouraged me, more than twenty five years ago, to wield my golf clubs again after they had learned the game from their grandparents.

Foreword

By Robert Trent Jones, Jr.

Dr. Leon White introduced me to *Golf Course of Rhymes* by describing it as "unique." And unique it is! Where else can you "play" a *Course* whose designers include the Duke of York (later King James II of England), Arthur Conan Doyle, Rudyard Kipling, British poet laureate John Betjeman, American poet laureate Billy Collins, U.S. Open Champion (1916) Charles "Chick" Evans as well as the great sports writers Grantland Rice and Ring Lardner? Yet, the *Course* is consistent with criteria I have used in designing critically acclaimed layouts such as Chambers Bay, Long Island National and the Poppy Hills Golf Club.

A great golf course, regardless of its style and setting, must be fun and playable. *Golf Course of Rhymes* certainly meets this test. No matter what your experience is with poetry, you will gain a new appreciation and zest for the game as you advance from "The Practice Tee" (the Introduction) to the course itself, which is made up of 18 Holes (Chapters), each with a theme that is dramatized with stories and poems. And when you reach the 19th Hole ("The Clubhouse") you will be rewarded with some of the funniest rhymes in the book. All of the *Course's* poetry is accessible, but as you might expect, some Holes will play a little harder than others.

Like the distinguishing characteristics of a great golf course, the stories and poems of *Golf Course of Rhymes* are memorable. No other course includes a poetic golf ball advertisement, the story of the first international golf match, golf's version of "Casey at the Bat," an epic poem matching a tipsy caddie and the Devil at St. Andrews, parodies of the *Rubaiyat* and a Hole devoted to "The Women's Game." In all, the *Course* includes more than 50 golf stories and 90 poems. For example, here are four lines boasting of golf's impact on health that appeared in the April 1916 issue of *The American Golfer* magazine:

It's the best exercise that a man ever had;
Take a fellow, run down, no matter how bad,
Eighteen holes—say, three times a week,
Will put pep in his blood and bronze on his cheek;

Dr. White, during his five years of research, discovered many of the *Course's* poems in rare golf books and magazines dating back to 1638 with most before 1930. In so doing he brought together more than 45 poets to help him construct his fanciful fairways and greens. As someone who thinks lyrically when designing a golf course, I can fully appreciate how well Dr. White has succeeded in his goal to again make playable a part of golf history and literature that is unknown to most of today's golfers.

So find a comfortable chair, head out to "The Practice Tee" and prepare to enjoy *Golf Course of Rhymes*, the best round of golf you will ever play without swinging a club.

Preface

The idea for this book began with a question: Is there a literature of golf poetry? I had written some golf poems without ever considering the possibility that other golfers, perhaps from earlier times, had had the same inclination. But one day, some years ago, I started thinking about this question. Fortunately, the Internet was available to help me find an answer.

I began my search for golf poetry by using the website, www.worldcat.org. Worldcat lets you use key words to roam the shelves of more than 10,000 libraries worldwide. I entered "golf poetry" and to my surprise found 99 English language entries. Publication dates ranged back to the 19th century, with the earlier books coming from England and Scotland. So the answer to my question was clearly "yes." But as I was to find out, the links between golf and poetry extend much further back in time and are not limited to books.

Historically, the first separately printed book devoted entirely to golf wasn't an instruction book, but rather a 358-line mock-epic poem called *The Goff* published in 1743! The first book to mention the game, *The Muses Threnodie,* was published a little more than a hundred years earlier in 1638. It, too, was a book of poetry.

The Internet led me to a second major source of golf poetry, English and American golf magazines of the late 19th and early 20th centuries. Some copies of these magazines have been digitized and are available on the United States Golf Association website. As an example of what I found, consider these lines from the November 1917 issue of *The American Golfer.*

"Here in America there has for long been the tendency in the game to versify. Our own pages . . . from time to time bear witness of it. Perhaps Grantland Rice [America's first great sports writer] has come nearest of all Americans to the true sentiment coupled with graceful phrasing . . . He has known that the truth can often be told in verse better than any other way. In his 'Dedication to the Duffer' at the beginning of *The Winning Shot*, and elsewhere in that book, there are some pretty pearls:

> This is the substance of our Plot—
> For those who play the Perfect Shot,
> There are ten thousand who do not.
> For each who comes to growl and whine
> Because one putt broke out of line
> And left him but a Sixty-Nine,
> At least ten thousand on the slate
> Rise up and cheer their blessed fate
> Because they got a Ninety-Eight.

In that, now there is very great truth indeed; is there not?"

So with the help of websites such as the USGA's www.usga.org, Worldcat.org and Google, I discovered a gold mine of golf poetry in old books and magazines.

The next step was to obtain copies of the books that looked the most interesting. That endeavor proved to be a challenge since most of the books were published more than eighty years ago. Moreover, from worldcat.org I found that many of the books were shelved in less than ten libraries in the U.S. However, with the help of the inter-library loan program, the Harvard University Library, eBay and PBA

Galleries, an auction house in San Francisco, I gained access to the books I was seeking.

Once I began reading the poetry in the books and golf magazines I quickly realized that, although the sources were old, the best of the poems were well worth preserving for a new generation of readers—thus, the genesis of this book. The fun, of course, began with the search for what poetry to include. But it extended also to the design of the book in the layout of a golf course and to the stories that link the poetry to related history, people and events.

I hope that you will enjoy reading the book as much as I have enjoyed putting it together. Don't hesitate to contact me at my blog, www.golfpoet.com, with your thoughts and observations.

Table of Contents

6th Hole. Great and Not So Great Moments   47

7th Hole. Parodies   57

8th Hole. Advice   77

xix

The Practice Tee

GOLFER. "What am I doing wrong now?"
INSTRUCTOR. "Standin' too near the ball—after you've hit it."

Surprising as it may seem, "golf poetry" is not a contradiction in terms. In earlier times, poetry was an integral part of the game's literature. In fact, the first separately printed book devoted entirely to golf, called *The Goff,* was a 358-line mock-epic poem initially published in 1743. The golf magazines of the late nineteenth and early twentieth centuries, such as *Golf, The Golfer, The American Golfer* and *Golf Illustrated & Outdoor America,* contained golf poems in almost every issue. Even a few advertisements contained poetry! Here is an example from a Spaulding golf ball ad titled "Driving Off on Parnassus" that appeared on the back cover of the August 1914 issue of *Golf Magazine:*

♦ *On Putting*

When the greens were fast and freakish,

Once my putts were either weakish
   Or absurdly strong.
Now I calmly snap my digits
For I play with
Spaulding "Midgets,"
   Not a putt goes wrong.

When a green's too hard for others,
Have recourse to Spaulding Brothers!
   Buy the perfect ball.
Architects may slope and ridge it,
But you'll always hole a "Midget,"
   And defeat them all.

Robert Frost was not threatened, and probably neither were Spaulding's competitors. But the fact that ad writers thought that rhymes could sell golf balls shows the degree to which poetry was part of the language of golf at this time.

Also in these earlier days, books entirely or partially devoted to golf poetry were published in Great Britain and the United States. Joseph S. F. Murdoch, a renowned golf book collector and bibliographer, wrote that "poetry made up most of the original writing on the game." He attributed this fact to the general popularity of poetry in the 19th century as a means for storytelling. Describing Scotland as a "nation of poets," Murdoch surmised,

> ". . . it is not difficult to believe that most of the early golf literature sprang from the lips of early after-dinner speakers who, lauding the merits of their national sport and finding some of their efforts enthusiastically received, printed the poems for distribution to their club-mates."

Golf Course of Rhymes brings to life again the wit, wisdom and golf sense of the best of these poet-golfers from this earlier time. Some of the poems offer advice on how to play a better game. Others entertain with humorous stories and tales. Still others focus on interesting historical themes. And a few even take on serious tones.

You may worry, however unnecessarily, that reading poetry presents a challenge as difficult as playing from the downhill slope of a deep bunker. Relax: the poetry in this book is understandable and engaging.

Think about reading and understanding a new poem as you might think about playing and understanding a hole on an unfamiliar golf course. The first time you play the hole you will try to grasp its general layout and develop an initial strategy for playing it from tee to green. In other words, the first time you play the hole you are trying to figure it out so that the next time you can play it better. The same thing is true with a poem.

The first time you read a poem you will get an idea of how it is structured and a general idea of how it moves from "tee" to "green." With most of the poems, full understanding will come with one reading. With an involved poem one reading may not leave you with a complete understanding of what the poet is trying to say. Just as the subtleties of a complex golf hole only become apparent after playing it more than once, so, too, with a more complicated poem. The fun with a challenging poem, as with a tricky hole, is in getting to know it through multiple experiences.

To play golf well you should swing your clubs with tempo, rhythm and timing. Reading poetry also requires tempo, rhythm and timing. These three qualities are best experienced by reading the poems out loud. And I would encourage you to read the poetry aloud in this book. You will definitely have more fun. To see what I mean, recite the following four lines written by a Scottish golfer that appeared in the December 1875 issue of *Blackwood's Edinburgh Magazine*:

> The apple-faced sage,
> With his nostrum for all,
> "Dinna hurry your swing!
> Keep your e'e on the ball!"

Your Scottish accent may need a little work, but I'm sure after a couple of readings you found a tempo, rhythm and timing that "felt" good. Not only that, you found out that your golf instructor's advice about slowing down your swing and keeping your head still is rather old news!

To increase confidence in your "swing," give the first stanza from a poem called "The Lay for the Troubled Golfer," written by an American golfer-poet Edgar A. Guest, born in 1881, the dramatic reading it deserves.

> His eye was wild and his face was taut with anger and
>   hate and rage,
> And the things he muttered were much too strong for
>   the ink of the printed page.
> I found him there when the dusk came down, in his golf
>   clothes still was he,
> And his clubs were strewn around his feet as he told his
>   grief to me:
> "I'd an easy five for a seventy-nine—in sight of the
>   golden goal—
> An easy five and I took an eight—an eight on the
>   eighteenth hole!

The lines in this poem are much longer than those in the first one. The tempo, rhythm and timing are different, but with a few readings you will get it. And I would be willing to bet that you had fun reading it out loud. The whole poem is included later on.

The joy, fascination, frustration, and love of the game of golf come through in the poetry of this book. Although some of the earlier poets played on natural fields where the only work done by the "architects" was to determine where to cut the holes and although their clubs were simpler and the balls were not high-tech, they loved playing golf at least as much as we do today. This passion comes through in their poetry.

In one of golf's earliest printed works, *A Few Rambling Remarks on Golf*, published in 1862, Robert Chambers begins, "Golf, or goff, is a pastime peculiar to Scotland." He expanded this thought in the golf section of a book called *Gymnastics, Golf and Curling*, which he published along with his brother in Edinburgh in 1866:

> "The game of Golf is believed to be peculiar to Scotland though most likely derived from Germany; the term *golf* being from the German word *kolbe* or the Dutch *kolf*, a club. The popular pronunciation of the Scotch word is *goff* or *gowf*."

Not surprisingly, therefore, Scottish golfers wrote most of the poetry in this book that predates 1900.

Later in *Gymnastics, Golf and Curling*, Chambers shows us how geographically local golf was in the early days when he suggest to his readers,

> "Procure a set of clubs from a good maker, such as M'Ewan of Musselburgh and Edinburgh; Morris, Brown, Wilson, or Gorgan of St. Andrews (Fife); Hunter of Blackheath (London), or Strath of Prestwick (Ayshire). Practise with short and stiff clubs at first, as they insure the steadiest play. Purchase a few

gutta-percha balls from trustworthy makers, such as
G. D. Brown or T. Morris. Put on shoes with strong
nails, to insure a firm footing on the grass; and if your
hands are tender, wear an old pair of kid gloves, of
not too tight a fit. You are now equipped, and may
proceed to the links."

Chambers was also a poet. Here is a verse he wrote
about the third hole at St. Andrews, from the poem, "The
Nine Holes of the Links of St. Andrews":

♦ The Third Hole

No rest in Golf—still perils in the path:
Here, playing a good ball, perhaps it goes
Gently into the *Principalian Nose*,
Or else *Tam's Coo* which equally is death.
Perhaps the wind will catch it in mid-air,
And take it to *the Whins*—"Look out, look out!
Tom Morris, be, oh be, a faithful scout!"
But Tom, though *links-eyed*, finds not anywhere.
Such thy mishaps, O Merit: feeble balls
Meanwhile roll on, and lie upon the green;
'Tis well, my friends, if you, when this befalls,
Can spare yourselves the infamy of spleen.
It only shows the ancient proverb's force,
That you may further go and fare the worse.

Chambers' experience is ours as well: good balls go astray
and are lost while "feeble balls" sometimes end up on the
green. But he wisely counsels: don't get angry; it could get
worse—advice offered more than a hundred years ago but still
relevant.

Those of you who have played the third hole at St. Andrew's Old Course may be a little confused by the bunker

references. At the time the poem was written, the Old Course, then the only course at St. Andrews, had only nine holes. Today the Principal's Nose is situated on the sixteenth hole which runs in the opposite direction, parallel to the third, and Tam's Coo has been filled in and no longer exists.

Golf's long and colorful history is well documented. Its origins, however, have always been uncertain. Sir Walter Simpson, an early golf historian, writes in *The Art of Golf*, published in 1887, that golf at St. Andrews probably began when a shepherd idly hit a stone into a hole with his crook. An anonymous 19th century poet gives us a charming poetic version of this apocryphal story.

> When Caledonia, stern and wild
> Was still a poor unkilted child,
> Two simple shepherds clad in skins,
> With leathern thongs about their shins,
> Finding that dullness day by day
> Grew irksome, felt a wish to play.
> But where the game? In those dark ages
> They couldn't toss—they had no wages.
> Till one, the brighter of the two,
> Hit on a something he could do.
> He hit a pebble with his crook
> And sent the stone across a brook;
> The other, tempted then to strike,
> With equal ardour "played the like,"
> And thus they went with heart and soul
> Towards a distant quarry-hole,
> > With new success contented
> > 'Twas thus the prehistoric Scot
> > Did wonders by an idle shot,
> > And golf was first invented.

Note the different rhythm, tempo and rhyme scheme in the last four lines of the poem, perhaps explaining why the poet indented his conclusion.

The first recorded mention of golf is in an Act of Parliament in 1457, in which King James II of Scotland attempted to ban the sport. From the 15th century until near the turn of the 20th century, golf was almost exclusively a British game. Since then, golf has become a major worldwide professional sport and a recreational activity for many millions of players. But for the individual golfer, the sensibilities of the game have changed little since the earliest days of golf. Golfing poets have expressed their thoughts, feelings and passions about the game of golf for more than three hundred years. The purpose of this book is to offer you an introduction to this largely unknown poetic treasure trove of the past augmented with contemporary poems and related stories and golf history.

The earliest song that mentions golf is a 17th century tune mentioned in the book *Poems on Golf* edited by Robert Clark and privately published in 1867 by members of The Edinburgh Burgess Golfing Society. The song is called "And to each pretty lass We will give a green gown" attributed by Clark to a poet named Thomas Shadwell. The original was discovered in a rare work entitled *Westminster Drollery*, published in 1671. The "scrap" included in Clark's book is as follows:

Thus all our life long we are frolick and gay,
And instead of Court revels, we merrily play
At Trap, at Rules, and at Barly-break run:
At GOFF, and at Foot-ball, and when we have done
These innocent sports, we'll laugh and lie down,
And to each pretty Lass
We will give a green Gown.

Not great poetry, but it marked a beginning.

The poems in the book are laid out along 18 Holes (Chapters). Some Holes will be longer and others shorter, some a little more difficult to get through and others pretty straightforward. And as with any good course, I have included a 19th Hole as well. Also, similar to the classic Scottish courses, each Hole has a name. For example, the 4th Hole is called "Agonies and Frustrations." As you might expect, it is one of the longer Holes!

Some poems in the book are too long to be included in their entirety. In these cases I have added text to describe what has been excluded and to explain the poem's nature and meaning. I also provide references so readers can find the complete poems.

Now as you head toward the 1st Hole, let me leave you with the "swing thought" for the book: read the poems out loud. If you do, I guarantee that you will get more enjoyment from playing this *Golf Course of Rhymes*.

1st Hole. Far and Sure

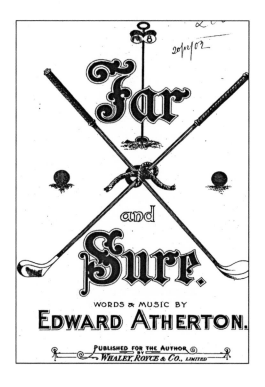

Today's golf equipment gives even average players the pleasure of hitting their drives "way out there" and in the fairway. Golfers in the early days had neither the clubs nor balls to hit mammoth drives. Nevertheless, distance and accuracy were also foremost in their thoughts and "Far and Sure" was the way they put it.

This motto was probably first seen on a plaque attached to the wall of John Patersone's house in the Canongate of Edinburgh in the mid-1680's. Earlier, in 1681, Patersone was just a poor shoemaker when the Duke of York (then King's Commissioner at Holyrood house in Scotland, later King

James II of England) chose him to be his partner in a stakes match pitting them against two English noblemen. This first international golf match was played over the Leith Links in Edinburgh, then a five hole course that dated back to at least 1552. The match was arranged to settle a disagreement between the Duke and his two English friends as to whether golf was an English or Scottish game. Needless to say, Patersone, a champion golfer highly familiar with the Links, and the Duke won for Scotland. Afterwards, Patersone built the Canongate house with his share of the winning purse, and the Duke supplied the plaque.

Almost two hundred years later, "Far and Sure" was immortalized again, this time in verses written by a poet golfer described only as "the late Sheriff Logan." The poem "Far and Sure" appears in Robert Clark's *Poems on Golf*. Who Sheriff Logan was remains a mystery, but clearly he was more than a lawman golfer. He must have been one of golf's early nineteenth hole philosophers! Note, however, that for Logan, "Far" referred to driving and "Sure" to putting, thus making the motto more all-encompassing.

♦ *Far and Sure*

"FAR and sure! far and sure!" 'twas the cry of our fathers,
 'Twas a cry which their forefathers heard;
'Tis the cry of their sons when the mustering gathers:
 When we're gone may it still be the word.

"Far and sure!" there is honour and hope in the sound;
 Long over these Links may it roll!
It will—O it will! For each face around
 Shows its magic is felt in each soul.

Let it guide us in life; at the desk or the bar,
 It will shield us from folly's gay lure;

Then, tho' rough be the course, and the winning-post *far*,
    We will carry the stakes—O be *sure!*

Let it guide us in Golf, whether "Burgess" or "Star;"
    At the last round let none look demure:
All Golfers are brothers when *driving* is *far*
    When putting is canny and *sure*.

"Far and sure! far and sure!" fill the bumper and drain it,
    May our motto for ever endure;
May time never maim it, nor dishonour stain it;
    Then drink, brothers, drink, "Far and sure!"

The next poem, also from Scotland, clearly old but of unknown origin, focuses on "The Golfer's Waggle." It makes reference to the motto while providing a catalogue of waggles that could only come from the mind of a golfing poet. It, too, has a philosophical flourish. This poem and some others to follow include Scottish dialect. Definitions when needed are appended to the right of the lines. The poem appeared in *The American Golfer* in September 1915.

♦ The Golfer's Waggle

Every golfer has a waggle—
A waggle o' his ain—*   of his own
A wiggle-waggle, long and short,
Wi' flourishes or plain.

The long and quick, the short and quick,
Long, short, and quick and slow;
The variety is infinite
That golfin' waggles show.

- 13 -

The sprightly waggle of success,
Dull waggle of defeat;
The weary waggle-wasting time,
The waggle of conceit.

The waggle of the swanky pro,
Of "Far and Sure" design;
The feeble waggle of old age,
That preludes "off the line."

The caddie's waggle-dry asides,
That golfers whiles maun* suffer;   must
And worst o' waggles on the links,
The waggle of the duffer.

The waggle shows the waggler,
Be the waggle slow or quick;
There is mair* into the waggle,   more
Than the waggle o' the stick.

    "Far and Sure" continues to appear in various golf guises. It is the motto of a number of golf clubs including the Royal Burgess Golfing Society of Edinburgh, the Royal Liverpool Golf Club at Hoylake, the North Wales Golf Club in Llandudno, the Chicago Golf Club and the Northeast Harbor Golf Club in Maine. The Coat of Arms of the Blairgowrie Golf Club in Scotland bears the inscription in Latin, "Longe Et Certe."

    The motto also shows up in a long forgotten 1902 song titled "Far and Sure," words and music by Edward Atherton, a Canadian song writer. Because golf was first played in Canada in Montréal in 1873, the motto obviously didn't take long to cross the ocean. The second verse will give you a sense that Atherton knew the game but that his song would not become golf's anthem.

Now to follow through is the thing to do
And to keep on the ball your eye,
Then a brassie shot to the wished-for spot
And your hopes are running high:
With your trusty cleek you have cleared the creek,
And you've reached the green in three.
One putt no more and you've holed in four,
How it fills your heart with glee!

Maybe after downing a sufficient amount of Scotch, a foursome could sing the following chorus in the "sprightly" manner suggested by its writer. The point to note is that by this time "Far and Sure" had probably run its course from Pattersone's plaque in the 1680's to Atherton's song in 1902, a good run to say the least.

Chorus:

Then hurrah! hurrah for the swing and drive,
Far and sure from the sandy tee.
With a caddie keen, and a well kept green,
"Far and Sure" is the game for me,
"Far and Sure" is the game for me.

"Far and sure" is the essential idea, but for the weekend player "far and wide" is more often the result of a hard swing with the driver. A Scottish caddie in the 1880's gave this advice to his wayward driving employer.

"Drive straucht, sir, that's the gran' thing. Ye see there's players that'll gae [go] tae [to] the richt, and syne [then] to the left; they'll go into the railway, and syne into the whins; but they canna [cannot] tak a doonricht straucht deleever [deliver a straight hit]. Now, sir, a doonricht straucht deleever is faur [far] better than a strappin' far shot. Play you straucht, sir, it's a hantle [a lot] better than playin' faur. And mind whaur [where] the bunkers lie, and keep oot o' them. A bunker's jeest tamnation to maist [most] players."

Now, as we putt out on this first hole, consider the observation made by the Chambers brothers, in their 1866 instruction book contrasting the importance of the long and short games.

"Much depends on [the] short game; and many a far, and even sure driver through the green, has been beaten by the indifferent swiper but deadly short-game player."

From the Chambers brothers to Dave Pelz, the message hasn't changed.

2nd Hole. St. Andrews

George Fullerton Carnegie, who played his golf at St. Andrews, Montrose, and Musselburgh, wrote and privately printed a small book of poetry in 1833 called *Golfiana or Niceties Connected with the Game of Golf . . . Dedicated, with Respect, to the Members of All Golfing Clubs, and to those of St. Andrews and North Berwick in Particular. Golfiana* is thought to be the next publication after *The Goff* entirely devoted to golf. This first edition included only one poem of 130 lines called "The Golfiad." According to Joseph Murdoch, only one copy of the first edition is known to exist. A second edition, which included two additional poems, "Address to St. Andrews" and "The First Hole at St. Andrews on a Crowded Day," was published later in 1833, this time for public sale. A third edition was published in 1842 with one more poem added, "Another Peep at the Links." This last edition of *Golfiana* was later republished in Clark's *Poems on Golf* (1867) and his *Golf* (1875), and in Stewart's *Golfiana Miscellanea* (1887). The PBA Galleries in San Francisco sold a "near fine" copy of the third edition of *Golfiana* at auction in July 2005 for $28,750.

Carnegie's fondness for both the town of St. Andrews and its historic course is evident in these beginning lines from "Address to St. Andrews":

> St. Andrews! they say that thy glories are gone,
> That thy streets are deserted, thy castles overthrown:
> If thy glories be gone, they are only methinks,
> As it were, by enchantment, transferr'd to thy Links.
> Though thy streets be not now, as of yore, full of prelates,
> Of abbots and monks, and of hot-headed zealots,
> Let none judge us rashly, or blame us as scoffers,
> When we say that instead there are Links full of Golfers.

And the "Address" ends with these wonderful four lines:

> If Golfers and caddies be not better neighbours
> Than abbots and soldiers, with crosses and sabres,
> Let such fancies remain with the fool who so thinks,
> While we toast old St Andrews, its Golfers and Links.

The religious references in the poem relate to the conflict caused by the Scottish Reformation of 1559 that led to Scotland becoming a Protestant state. The description of the town and toast makes more sense when we learn that the city of St. Andrews, the former ecclesiastical capital of Scotland, and its great University were in rapid decline by the early 19th century. By the middle of the century that city was "in danger of extinction altogether." St. Andrews was saved, however, both by the game of golf and by a major modernization effort that was set in motion by Sir Hugh Lyon Playfair, an early captain of the Royal and Ancient Golf Club of St. Andrews.

According to the highly respected Scottish golf historian Robert Browning (not the famous Victorian poet), the first golf club to be established was the Honourable Company of Edinburgh Golfers, whose start he dates as March 7, 1744. When club members began playing, they played on the Leith Links, where John Patersone and the Duke of York had teamed up for their famous match about sixty years earlier. The Golf Club of St. Andrews came into existence ten years later, May 14, 1754. Browning identifies the Honourable Company of Golfers at Blackheath, today located in Eltham, England, as the first golf club organized outside of Scotland. It began on August 16, 1766. Although the Golf Club at St. Andrews was not formed until 1754, evidence exists that some form of golf was played in the town as early as January 25, 1552. Eighty years after the St. Andrews club began, in 1834, the title "Royal and Ancient Golf Club" was bestowed on St. Andrews by King William IV.

In the third poem of *Golfiana*, "The First Hole at St. Andrews on a Crowded Day," Carnegie refers to a number of well-known players of his time, including Hugh Lyon Playfair, the town's savior mentioned above:

See Colonel Playfair, shaped in form *rotund*,
Parade the unrivall'd Falstaff of the ground;
He laughs and jokes, play "what you like," and yet
You'll rarely find him make a foolish bet.

Carnegie also writes about a caddie named Davie. Davie is David Robertson, the father of the first great professional golfer, Allan Robertson. Starting at line fifteen:

For instance—Davie, oldest of the cads,
Who gives *half-one* to unsuspicious lads,
When he *might* give them *two* or even *more*,
And win, perhaps, three matches out of four,
Just as politic in *his* affairs
As Talleyrand or Metternich in *theirs.*
He has the statesman's elements, 'tis plain,
Cheat, flatter, humbug—*anything* for gain;
And had he trod the world's wide field, methinks,
As long as he has trod St. Andrews Links,
He might have been prime minister, or priest,
My lord, or plain *Sir David* at the least.

In "Another Peep at the Links," the poem Carnegie added in the third edition of *Golfiana,* he connects the father and the son:

Great Davie Robertson, the eldest cad,
In whom the good was stronger then the bad;
He sleeps in death! and with him sleeps a skill,
Which Davie, statesmanlike, could wield at will!
Sound be his slumbers! Yet if he should wake
In worlds where golf is played, himself he'd shake,
And look about, and tell each young beginner.
"I'll gie half-ane—nae mair*, [I'll give half-one—no
      more] as I'm a sinner."
He leaves a son, and Allan is his name,
In golfing far beyond his father's fame;
Tho' in diplomacy, I shrewdly guess,
His skill's inferior, and his fame is less.

As with the "Address to St. Andrews," Carnegie again ends his poem poignantly:

And now farewell! I am the worse for wear—
Grey is my jacket, growing grey my hair!

And though my play is pretty much the same,
Mine is, at best, a despicable game.
But still I like it—still delight to sing
Clubs, players, caddies, balls, and everything.
But all that's bright must fade! and we who play,
Like those before us, soon must pass away;
Yet it requires no prophet's skill to trace
The royal game thro' each succeeding race;
While on the tide of generations flows,
It still shall bloom, a never-fading rose;
Still St Andrews Links, with flags unfurl'd,
Shall peerless reign, and challenge all the world!

Carnegie died in 1851 at the age of fifty-one.

Worth noting is that Allan Robertson seems to have the distinction of being the first "greatest golfer of all times." At the time of his death in September 1859, an article in the *Dundee Advertiser* described Robertson as "the greatest golf-player that ever lived, of whom alone in the annals of the pastime it can be said that he never was beaten . . ." Robertson died a little more than one hundred years after the start of the Golf Club of St. Andrews. In this period, the number of golf clubs in Scotland had only risen to nineteen.

This Hole concludes with a poem by Robert Trent Jones, Jr., best known as one of the greatest contemporary golf architects but also regarded as a fine amateur poet.

♦ *Saint Andrews*

Round and round we go
   in the calm and in the gale
   gentle air suddenly impaled.
Round and round we go
   always back as first I came
   among true spirits of the game.

A barren, timeless land tolled by bells,
Carved by wind and shepherds on watch,
Given to humble folk by noblesse oblige,
A low links from receding seas;
They walked the crook rounded at the estuary.
By ancient and royal measure, 83 acres without a tree
Evolving to 18 shots of whisky and holes of golf
A field of such complexity;
With but 11 greens and 9 fairways
The Old Course confounds to create,
A profound test for all full rounds.

Friends have passed by friends
For half a millennium in all seasons
Inhaling pure air at Sea's end.
In summer, full joy at the long solstice light,
In winter, girded against the cold wind and early night,
The same friends passed by unrecognized
Except by the manner of the others' swing and stride.
Unseen bunkers evoked anger and mirth
For tall and slim or stout of girth.

Baptized upon our journey begun,
When life and all is lost and won,
Return we from whence we came.
Again the wee burn bids us in faith to cross
To safe home as did St. Andrews upon his cross.

Round and round we go
    in the calm and in the gale
    gentle air suddenly impaled.
Round and round we go
    always back as first I came
    among true spirits of the game.

3rd Hole. Joys of Golf

Arthur Conan Doyle is best known as the creator of the greatest fictional detective of the 19th century, Sherlock Holmes. Doyle, born in Scotland in 1859, was also a lifelong golfer who loved the game. He lived for many years next to the Crowborough Beacon Golf Club in Sussex, England, where he was a member. When writing his detective stories, he could look up from his desk and out onto the course. Doyle was his club's captain in 1910. His wife, following in his footsteps the next year, was captain of the "lady's section." Although he did not write about golf in his books, Doyle made his poetical statement about the joys of the game in a poem called "A Lay of the Links." ("Lay" in Doyle's day meant a ballad or song.) The poem was first published in 1898 in a book of Doyle's poetry called *Songs of Action* and then appeared in October 1909 in *The American Golfer*. Amazon.com (U.K) lists it as a golf song with music by Aubrey Yorke and words by Doyle, published in 1895.

♦ *A Lay of the Links*

It's up and away from our work to-day,
   For the breeze sweeps over the down;
And it's hey for a game where the gorse blossoms flame,
   And the bracken is bronzing to brown.
With the turf 'neath our tread and the blue overhead,
   And the song of the lark in the whin;
There's the flag and the green, with the bunkers between—
   Now will you be over or in?

The doctor may come, and we'll teach him to know
   A tee where no tannin can lurk;
The soldier may come, and we'll promise to show
   Some hazards a soldier may shirk;
The statesman may joke, as he tops every stroke,
   That at last he is high in his aims;
And the clubman will stand with a club in his hand
   That is worth every club in St. James'.

The palm and the leather come rarely together,
   Gripping the driver's haft,
And it's good to feel the jar of the steel
   And the spring of the hickory shaft.
Why trouble or seek for the praise of a clique?
   A cleek here is common to all;
And the lie that might sting is a very small thing
   When compared with the lie of the ball.

Come youth and come age, from the study or stage,
   From Bar or from Bench—high and low!
A green you must use as a cure for the blues—
   You drive them away as you go.

We're outward bound on a long, long round,
    And it's time to be up and away:
If worry and sorrow come back with the morrow,
    At least we'll be happy to-day.

If you have ever played on a links course in the British Isles, you will appreciate the next poem, "Seaside Golf," by John Betjeman, an English Poet Laureate and well known radio and television personality in Britain in the 1960's and 70's. Finding a poem that better expresses the personal joys of playing golf would be a difficult task. It is only fitting then that Betjeman's final resting place is a simple grave on the grounds of St. Enodoc Church in the South West of England, among the sand dunes facing the 10th fairway of his favorite course. In fact the 10th through 14th holes of the St. Enodoc links form a circle around the 11th century Church.

♦ Seaside Golf

How straight it flew, how long it flew,
It clear'd the rutty track
And soaring, disappeared from view
Beyond the bunker's back—
A glorious, sailing, bounding drive
That made me glad I was alive.

And down the fairway, far along
It glowed a lonely white;
I played an iron sure and strong
And clipp'd it out of sight,
And spite of grassy banks between
I knew I'd find it on the green.

And so I did. It lay content
Two paces from the pin;

A steady putt and then it went
Oh, most surely in.
The very turf rejoiced to see
That quite unprecedented three.

Ah! Seaweed smells from sandy caves
And thyme and mist in whiffs,
In-coming tide, Atlantic waves
Slapping the sunny cliffs,
Lark song and sea sounds in the air
And splendour, splendour everywhere.

The next poem, "On Course," also portrays the joys and pleasures of playing golf but uses a more modern free-verse form.

◆ On Course

Golf is a singular way
to take temporary leave
following a zigzag path
in search of a small white ball;

to abandon reality,
but stay the course,
hole after hole;

to create a new story,
always different
to be told to someone
before it's forgotten.

An extraordinary chance
to pretend for a brief time
no matter how unskilled
that each stroke will be flawless;

to endure the pain of failure
without really failing,
and even if only once a round,

to truly enjoy
the pure pleasure
of hitting the ball rock-solid
or sinking a long tricky putt.

In the poem above, I point to the uniqueness of golf as a
source of pleasure and joy to golfers. "The Perfect Golfer" in
John E. Baxter's book *Locker Room Ballads*, published in 1923,
would have understood.

♦ The Perfect Golfer

His drives are rather ragged and his iron shots are punk;
His putting's an amazing thing; he's rarely ever sunk
A putt much longer that a foot; his mashie stroke's a sin;
Somehow he can't seem to get a touch of Hagen spin
To hold it safely on the green; his brassie shot's the type
The devil teaches when the lads are slightly under-ripe.
And more than that he knows all traps; not one but has its
    charms
And welcomes him with encores and, it seems, with
    outstretched arms;
But somehow it can't feaze him much; a song is in his heart
And on his lips a whistle and a jest of golfing art.
When he comes in he always has the graciousness to say
"This Club is perfect, I have had a most delightful day."
And though we jest and laugh at him, we'll tell the wide world
    flat
God made the golf course brighter when he made a man like
    that.

The perfect golfer actually spoke for himself a few years earlier at the beginning of a column by "Bunker Hill" from the May 1915 issue of *The American Golfer.*

My drive is erratic, my brassie's the same,
My irons are atrocious, and awful my aim,
My mashie is tearful, my putting worse still,
My scores have the look of a dressmaker's bill;
My legs are a-weary, my wrists are quite lame,
But I am most happy—I'm playing the game.

4th Hole. Agonies and Frustrations

"Having no spade, partner?"

The name of this hole could serve as the title of the following short poem said to be from *Auld Wullie's Almanack*, dated 1623:

> I feel particularly fit today,
> Keen is the green unclouded are the heavens.
> And yet there's summat wrong; the holes I play
> Are all at saxes when they're not at seven.

It is unlikely, however, that the poem was written in the early 1600's, since at that time medal play scoring was not a part of the game. Again quoting the Scottish golf historian Robert Browning,

"In the early days of golf the only form of play was the match between two opposing sides, decided by holes. What seems the simple and obvious plan of counting the number of each player's strokes had never suggested itself to the minds of the followers of the game, and even the tally of strokes at each hole was kept by a purely relative method of computation."

Nevertheless, the poem is timeless. Who has not gone out on a beautiful day feeling "particularly fit" and then proceeded to play horribly? The poet that wrote these distressing four lines still speaks for us.

Moreover, for a description of pain and grief that only golfers can understand, consider reciting the first two stanzas of E. M. Griffiths' poem, "O, Who Would Court?" The poem appeared in *With Club and Caddie*, published in London in 1909.

♦ *O, Who Would Court?*

O who would court the golfer's pain,
The wary waggle wagged in vain,
The gust that takes the ball again,
    The execrable lie,
The yielding sand, the bunker's slope,
The rising score and sinking hope,
The wrath unfettered in its scope
    When severed club-heads fly;

The grief that in the breast is wrought
By an approach shot just too short,
The ball irrevocably caught
    In broken ground or whin*,   gorse or high grass
The putt, which while it seems to roll
Dead—as a magnet to the pole

Stops scarce two inches from the hole,
   And lets the opponent in.

Is there a more vivid two-line description of a struggling bunkered golfer than, "The yielding sand, the bunker's slope/ The rising score and sinking hope?"

Andrew Lang, born in 1844, was educated at both St. Andrews and Oxford universities and was one of the ablest and most versatile writers of his day. He published a large number of books of poetry as well as novels and books on Scottish history. His writings on golf include both several chapters in *A Batch of Golfing Papers* published in 1892 and the introductory chapter, "The History of Golf" in Horace Hutchinson's highly regarded Badminton Library book *Golf*, published in 1890. In addition, Lang wrote a number of golf poems. In the following lament, he makes clear that the agonies and frustrations of playing golf have a long history.

♦ *Off my Game*

"I'm off my game," the golfer said,
And shook his locks in woe;
"My putter never lays me dead,
My drives will never go;
Howe'er I swing, howe'er I stand,
Results are still the same,
I'm in the burn*, I'm in the sand—   brook
I'm off my game!

"Oh, would that such mishaps might fall
On Laidlay or Macfie,
That they might toe or heel the ball,
And sclaff* along like me!   hit behind the ball
Men hurry from me in the street,
And execrate my name,

Old partners shun me when we meet—
I'm off my game!

"Why is it that I play at all?
Let memory remind me
How once I smote upon my ball,
And bunkered it—BEHIND ME.
I mostly slice into the whins*,   gorse or high grass
And my excuse is lame—
It cannot cover half my sins—
I'm off my game!

"I hate the sight of all my set,
I grow morose as Byron*;   English poet
I never loved a brassey yet,
And now I hate an iron.
My cleek seems merely made to top,
My putting's wild or tame;
It's really time for me to stop—
I'm off my game!"

In the poem, Laidlay refers to Johnny Laidlay, the Amateur Champion in 1889 and 1891, and Macfie to Allan Macfie, who won the first Amateur Championship in 1885.

How many times after playing a hole poorly, being "off your game," have you said to yourself, "If only I could play that hole again?" Here are some verses I wrote regarding such a replay:

♦ *If only I could play that hole again*

If only I could play that hole again
I know that I could shoot a better score
That drive I hit was rather short and right
A second chance would let me make a four.

Instead my second shot is from the trees
It traveled only fifty yards at best
And left me feeling sick and ill at ease.

I'm sure if asked my teacher would agree
With all the skill I have but have not shown
I should be lining up a putt for three.

Instead I have a tricky wood to play
A side-hill up-hill lie around a bend
A perfect shot would show that I'm okay.

My swing is perfect but the ball went wide
It disappeared from sight and was not found
Nothing I can do will turn the tide.

Instead of two I'm on the green in six
My second putt lips out my score is nine
Bad luck it is that put me in this fix.

I'd really like to play that hole again
To show off all my talent and my skill
My partners think my attitude is great
But check my chance to make a par as nil.

For an elite player in earlier times or even today, nothing can be more frustrating than coming close but never winning a major event. That's the challenge that Charles "Chick" Evans, Jr. faced for a number of years after becoming a leading amateur player in America. Evans lost in the semifinals of the National Amateur Championship three years in a row, 1909–1911. In the January 1912 issue of *The American Golfer*, Evans showed that at least he could beat his English rivals Vardon, Taylor and Braid with his poetry (see the 10th Hole for confirmation), publishing his woes in these cleverly written verses:

◆ A Chronic Semi-Finalist

I'm a semi-final hoodoo,
    I'm afraid
I can never do as you do,
    Jimmie Braid*;   five time Open Champ
I've a genius not to do it,
I excel at almost to it,
But I never can go through it,
    I'm afraid.

I have seen how Hilton* plays it,   great English amateur
    I, dismayed,
And each problem how he weighs it,
    Unafraid.
Straight he goes for woe, or weal,
And his nerves are bits of steel
Made to work and not to feel,
    Thus he played.

Now it's just as plain as can be,
    I can't putt,
So I must an also-ran be
    In a rut.
Hilton! Could I do as you do!
Oh, a mascot for my hoodoo!
Travis*, tell me how 'tis you do   great American amateur
    That small putt.

 So this is a heartfelt cry
    Of my muse.
Fate, I beg you hear my sigh,
    Don't refuse.
I ask not the nation's prize,
But the finals tempt my eyes,
Halfway-finals I despise

When I lose.

Oh! A mascot, for I'm ever
    One of four;
Quatrefoil and horse-shoe never
    Bring me more.
A new mascot do I need,
Hoodoo-proof and guaranteed
To the finals it will lead,
    Nothing more.

Unfortunately, in the 1913 National Amateur Championship, Evans lost again in the semifinals. Later, writing his impressions of the tournament in the October 1913 issue of the magazine *Golf*, Evans observed:

"My greatest and most lasting impression . . . is that [the Championship] represented Opportunity No. 5 thrown away by me . . . It emphasized once more the strange fate that annually destroys me, usually on the afternoon half of the 36-hole semi-final round of the National Championship. This chronic happening is tragic or comic, as one chances to view it . . ."

In Chick's case, as the poem indicates, he chose the comic perspective.

Happily, though not immediately, Evan's luck changed. In 1916 he became the first golfer to win both the National Amateur and the U.S. Open Championship in the same year. The only other golfer to achieve this feat was Bobby Jones in 1930 when he won the Grand Slam. Evans is also remembered for competing in a record fifty amateur championships in a row. Today his name is associated with the Evans Scholars Foundation, which he started in 1930, that offers deserving caddies the chance to go to college.

Edgar Albert Guest, born in England in 1881, worked for *The Detroit Free Press* more than sixty years. For more than half that time, a poem written by Guest appeared in the paper every day it went to press. His most popular collection of poetry, *A Heap o' Livin,'* sold more than a million copies. As we could have sympathized with Chick Evans, we can all commiserate with Guest's "Troubled Golfer."

◆ *The Lay for the Troubled Golfer*

His eye was wild and his face was taut with anger and hate and
    rage,
And the things he muttered were much too strong for the ink of
    the printed page.
I found him there when the dusk came down, in his golf clothes
    still was he,
And his clubs were strewn around his feet as he told his grief to
    me:
"I'd an easy five for a seventy-nine—in sight of the golden
    goal—
An easy five and I took an eight—an eight on the eighteenth
    hole!

"I've dreamed my dreams of the 'seventy men,' and I've worked
    year after year,
I have vowed I would stand with the chosen few ere the end of
    my golf career;
I've cherished the thought of a seventy score, and the days have
    come and gone
And I've never been close to the golden goal my heart was set
    upon.
But today I stood on the eighteenth tee and counted that score
    of mine,
And my pulses raced with the thrill of joy—I'd a five for

seventy-nine!

"I can kick the ball from the eighteenth tee and get this hole in
 five,
But I took the wood and I tried to cross that ditch with a mighty
 drive—"
Let us end the quotes, it is best for all to imagine his language
 rich,
But he topped that ball, as we often do, and the pill stopped in
 the ditch.
His third was short and his fourth was bad and his fifth was off
 the line,
And he took an eight on the eighteenth hole with a five for a
 seventy-nine.

I gathered his clubs and I took his arm and alone in the locker
 room
I left him sitting upon the bench, a picture of grief and gloom;
And the last man came and took his shower and hurried upon
 his way,
But still he sat with his head bowed down like one with a mind
 astray,
And he counted his score card o'er and o'er and muttered this
 doleful whine:
"I took an eight on the eighteenth hole, with a five for a seventy-
 nine!"

At the 2009 British Open at Turnberry, Tom Watson
needed a four on the final hole to win his sixth Open championship. Unfortunately he didn't do it. Thus, he lost his chance
to make history as the oldest golfer to win a major. He was 59
at the time. Shortly after, I wrote the following poem to pay
tribute to Watson's heroic but failed effort.

◆Watson At Turnberry – The 2009 Open

From the tee at eighteen
He looked down towards the home hole
Like a pitcher with a one run lead looks
Toward home plate needing one more out.

As he drove his ball
We knew what the magic number was.
When the camera showed a safe white speck
We exhaled in unison and counted one.

Now it was an eight iron to the green
Or was it a nine?
A question to be answered twice,
The first time by Watson alone.

He was thinking nine but hit the eight
And as we watched with growing anxiety
The ball bounced hard and rolled too far.
We held our breath and counted two.

Again a choice: to chip or putt.
One of the best chippers of all time,
The words of an old pro in the booth.
But the third stroke would be a putt.

From off the green the ball raced up
Then by the hole a good eight feet.
He said he had seen grain.
Down to one, we saw trouble.

Once more a putt to win the Open,
But this was not a kid with a dream
This was a Champion Golfer five times over.
Yet now we feared the worst.

While he took two short practice strokes
We lost interest in counting
And as the ball rolled weakly off his putter
We lost all hope as well.

I made a lousy putt, Watson's words;
Then it was one bad shot after another.
A self-stated epitaph marked the close:
The Old Fogy Almost Did It.

And so the golf writers lost their story
To an illustrious sage from an earlier time.
It wouldn't be about Watson winning – or losing,
But how he had played the Game.

As a lighthearted response to the golf poetry of agony and frustration, amply illustrated above, and as a way to reinforce the positive golfing attitude I took so many years to develop, I wrote the following:

♦ *Golf Sense*

Is there a golfer who's happy
content with his score and his game,
a partner who after losing a hole
is willing to share in the blame?

Is there a golfer who's tough enough
to manage his ego and say:
"My driver is totally out of control,
I'll hit my three-wood today?"

Is there a golfer who when asked
"How is your putting these days?"
doesn't respond with a terrible tale

but answers with nothing but praise?

Is there a golfer after a round
where he's missed his score by a mile
that describes the disaster hole by hole
and does it all with a smile?

Is there a golfer anywhere
who always takes dead aim
and does so pretending seriousness
knowing golf's only a game?

5th Hole. Golf as a Cure for What Ails You

"The Links of Innerleven" is a poem of six eight-line stanzas that was sung at the autumn meeting of the Innerleven Golf Club in 1841. Its first four lines provide an early prescription of golf as a cure for what ails you:

Wha wad* be free from doctor's bills—   *Who would*
From trash o'powders and o'pills—
Will find a cure for a' his ills
On the links o' Innerleven.

In a short piece titled "Golf at Seventy," written in 1863, a golfing writer begins,

"The effects of a game at golf on the body, and the mind, require to be felt to be appreciated. Such is the healthy and invigorating effect of exercise that it is no unusual thing for its votaries to play till they have exceeded the allotted three-score and ten. Those hale old gentlemen who ornament the golfing green (long may they continue to do so!), how deeply they enjoy themselves; how ruddy their cheek and bright their eye, when on the close of a bracing day in autumn

they come in from the enjoyment of their daily round!
Golf, thou art a gentle spirit; we owe thee much . . ."

In reading the above, remember that in the 1860's there were
no golf carts or trolleys, only perambulation and caddies.

A skeptic who signed his poem "By the Oil Man," wrote
these lines that appeared in the April 1916 issue of *The American Golfer*:

When my friend used to talk about golf to me
I always answered complacently:
"Oh, the game's all right for the old and fat—
For Carnegie, Taft and for folks like that;

Then he got "The Golf Bug," the name of the poem, and
with his new and enthusiastic view of the game:

It's the best exercise that a man ever had;
Take a fellow, run down, no matter how bad,
Eighteen holes—say, three times a week,
Will put pep in his blood and bronze on his cheek;

The Oil Man clearly saw golf as a cure for what ails you!

Here are three more examples, from early golf magazines. First, from a 1906 issue of *Golf Illustrated*:

There is an old person of Bickley
Who for sixty long years had been sickly,
    Since taking up golf
    His ailments are off,
He's renewing his youth very quickly.

Here are a quick four lines from an 1893 issue of *Golf*:

To drive the Golf ball on the ground,
To spoon it o'er the hill,
Will keep both mind and body sound,
And save the doctor's bill.

And in another issue of *Golf*, later the same year, a poem "A Song of Golf" included the following healthful and colorful stanza:

When doctors fail to cure you, and you go from bad to
    worse,
Your head just like a toy shop, and existence but a
    curse,
You need not knuckle under, be it fever, chill, or cough,
Just take your clubs and caddie, and then whack away at
    Golf.
        Then whack away at Golf,
        Then smack away at Golf,
You can banish pills and potions if you whack away at
    Golf.

Predating all of the above but similar in thought, a song called "The Golfer's Garland," composed for the Blackheath Golf Club before 1793, intones the praises of golf with both spirit and poignancy.

◆ The Golfer's Garland

Of rural diversions too long has the Chace*   Chase
All the honours usurp'd, and assum'd the chief place;
But truth bids the Muse from henceforward proclaim,
That GOFF, first of sports, shall stand foremost in fame.

O'er the Heath, see our heroes in uniform clad,
In parties well match'd, how they gracefully spread;
While with long strokes and short strokes they tend to the Goal,

And with putt well directed plump into the hole.

Goff we contend without rancour or spleen,
And bloodless the laurels we reap on the green;
From vig'rous exertions our raptures arise,
And to crown our delights no poor fugitive dies.

From exercise keen, from strength active and bold,
We'll traverse the green, and forget we grow old;
Blue Devils, diseases, dull sorrow and care,
Knock'd down by our Balls as they whiz thro' the air.

Health, happiness, harmony, friendship, and fame,
Are the fruits and rewards of our favourite game.
A sport so distinguish'd the Fair must approve:
Then to Goff give the day, and the ev'ning to love.

Our first standing toast we'll to Goffing assign,
No other amusement's so truly divine;
It has charms for the aged, as well as the young,
Then as first of field sports let its praises be sung.

The next we shall drink to our friends far and near,
And the mem'ry of those who no longer appear;
Who have play'd their last round, and pass'd over
    that bourne*   boundary
From which the best Goffer can never return.

"Blue devils, diseases, dull sorrow and care" may be "knock'd down by our balls as they whiz thro' the air." They might even be temporarily knocked out, if one of those balls lands in the hole. Needless to say, when I made a hole-in-one some years ago, it made me feel ecstatic for some time. I recorded my good fortune poetically, using "Stopping by Woods on a Snowy Evening" by Robert Frost as the model.

◆ *A Good Walk Unspoiled* – October 1, 2003
(With apologies to Robert Frost and Mark Twain)

I hit a ball into the sky
I hit it from a perfect lie
From tee to pin one-sixty-four
If just to there the ball would fly.

I've hit few balls like that before
On line that orb did deftly soar
It sailed just like a diamond kite
How could I really ask for more?

Then on the green it did alight
But soon it disappeared from sight
I started walking towards the pole
Where did the golf ball end its flight?

Not in the trap, not by the knoll
Not on the green, but in the hole!
And on my card I wrote a one
And on my card I wrote a one.

6th Hole. Great and Not-So-Great Moments

The PGA.com headline read "The Chip Heard 'Round the World.'" The shot, of course, was Tiger Woods' chip from behind the sixteenth green on the final day of the 2005 Masters. Art Spander, an *Oakland Tribune*'s golf writer at the time, remembered the event later in the year:

> "The images, so poignant, so enthralling, stay with us even now, months after they were created on that momentous Sunday in April."

As the months have now turned to years, I tried to recapture those images and reactions with a poem:

◆ *A Masters Chip for the Ages*

From a difficult lie beyond
the steeply sloped sixteenth green

a steely-eyed Tiger sent his ball
to a spot far above the hole,

the ball coming crisply off his wedge,
flew low, bounced once

and rolled on a yard or two
until gravity took over,

causing it to turn sharply,
and start slowly down the slope

towards the hole, speeding up
then slowing again as it got closer.

All of a sudden, Tiger's words,
it looked really good . . .

how could it not go in, and
when it stopped, a single turn short,

how did it not go in,
and all of a sudden it went in.

It was as if Tiger's will
had given gravity an assist.

In your life, the tower announcer's voice,
have you seen anything like that?

While around him, the patrons' roar
rose rocket-like, fueled by sheer wonder.

About 115 years earlier, on December 10, 1890, with almost no one watching, George Wright, later a baseball Hall-
of-Famer, and three friends played the first round of golf ever

in Boston. Wright, baseball player turned golfer, created the first great moment for New England golf. Earlier, in 1871, with his baseball career over, Wright, along with Henry Ditson, formed the sporting goods company, Wright and Ditson. Their company was bought out by A. G. Spalding & Co. in the early 1890's. Up to the buyout, Wright and Ditson had imported all of its golf merchandise from Scotland. Later, Spalding & Co. began producing its own clubs under both the Spalding and the Wright and Ditson names. George Wright's accomplishments moved me to write a poem commemorating him:

♦ George Wright (1847–1937)

He never had an equal as a fielder
He ran the bases better than the rest
As a hitter he was feared and fearless
In his time George Wright was unsurpassed.

In '69 he played for Cincinnati
Standing out at bat and on the field
He revolutionized the play at shortstop
And hit .633 which was unreal.

From Cincinnati he moved on to Boston
The Stockings first, the Red Caps later on
He led the mighty Sox to four straight pennants
Then with the Caps another two he won.

His ball field feats were cheered by all who saw him
He was an early hero of the game
Still it took the voters until thirty-seven
To elect him to the Baseball Hall of Fame.

Wright the player is today all but forgotten

But with regard to fame another claim
Retired from the ball field but still active
He brought to town the great old Scottish game.

A permit from the Boston Parks Commission
Let Wright lay out some holes at Franklin Park
Then on a cold fall day in eighteen ninety
He took along three pals to play 'til dark.

So add the name George Wright to your sports heroes
A pioneer in not one sport but two
The father of the golf game in New England
A double Hall-of-Famer through and through.

Unfortunately, not-so-great moments have their place in golf history as well. In 1970, Doug Sanders, described by Golf Hall-of-Famer Johnny Miller as "a crowd-pleasing showman who dressed loud, lived fast and made golf the glamour game it was in the 1960s and '70s," missed a short, crucial putt on the eighteenth green at the British Open. The following poem memorializes this famous run-by that cost Sanders the tournament.

♦ An Open Putt Remembered

The putt was less than three feet long
Just how could anything go wrong?

For sure he knew the stakes were high
But could he really run it by?

Doug looked as cool as cool could be
His poise was there for all to see.

But as his putter made its sweep
And those who watched made not a peep.

The ball escaped its aimed-for goal
And did not end up in the hole.

The question was, how could he miss
An easy putt as short as this?

The answer—simple, known to all:
Pressure putts don't always fall.

Not-so-great moments can also be both more mundane
and less consequential, the kind the happen to us. One such
situation is captured succinctly by J. H. Smith in Henry
Litchfield West's book, *Lyrics of the Links*, published in 1921.

♦ Early Golf

Course heavy,
    Grass wet,
Slip, slide,
    Cuss, fret.

Game over,
    Got beat,
Bad case
    Cold feet.

Pay caddie,
    Pay bet,
Run home
    And forget.

Next day,
    As before,
Back again,
    For more.

When it comes to sports poetry, without a doubt, the number one not-so-great moment belongs to the mighty Casey. "Casey at the Bat" was written in 1888 by 1885 Harvard graduate Ernest Thayer. In June 1909, the magazine *The American Golfer* published a golf sequel called "Hoo Andra Foozled Oot" ("How Andrew Foozled Out") by Tom Bendelow.

Bendelow was born in Aberdeen, Scotland in 1868 and immigrated to the United States in 1892. Far from famous as a poet, Bendelow was nicknamed "The Johnny Appleseed of American Golf," noting the fact that he designed at least 480 and possibly as many as 1000 golf courses during his lifetime. He is best remembered as the original architect of the South course at Olympia Fields and Medinah's Course #3, both in Illinois, and the East Lake Golf Club in Georgia, original home course to Bobby Jones and recent venue for professional golf's playoff ending Tour Championship.

Starting in 1899, Bendelow redesigned the first nine holes at the country's first municipal golf course, Van Courtland Park in New York City. Later he designed and oversaw the addition of a second nine. He is also credited with opening the first indoor golf instructional school at New York City's Carnegie Hall in 1895! For the first two decades of the 20th century, he was employed as a golf course designer by A.G. Spalding who saw golf course expansion as the best way to increase sales of his clubs and balls.

Now on to Tom Bendelow's dramatic poem.

◆ *Hoo Andra Foozled Oot*

The links were bricht an' bonnie
    Wi' tartan an' wi' plaid,
When the pride o' Skeebo village*   golf's Mudville
    Play'd the best that Cleveland haid.

The play was fast and furious
    As soon's the ba' was thwack'd,
But in the final test o' skill
    Ae' point oor Andra' lack'd.*   A point our Andrew lacked

The caddies stood wi' bated breath
    An' every ee* was set,   eye
For no a mon was in that crood
    But had his sillerd* bet.   money

Ae' caddie cried as wi' his club
    Oor Andra' faced the ba'
"Hoot, mon, play up, and show them noo*   now
    Hoo* Skeebo beats them a'."   how

Oor John he never winked an ee
    Nae maitter fat* they said,   No matter what
He kent* old Andra's game gey* well knew   rather
    An' it never fashed* his head.   bothered

He kent that a' he had tae dae
    Was play a waiting game,
Sae a' he did wis cracked a joke
    Wi' him o' library fame.

A' even at the seventeenth hole
    Was hoo the game did stand
When Andra' stepped up tae the tee
    Wi' driver in his haun'.

Oor Andra look'd up at the sky,
    An' then doon at the dirt
An' cannily* he weigh'd his club   carefully
    An' loos'd his pleated shirt.

An' then he plaintit baith his feet,
    An' syne* replantit each,   then

An' swung his club St. Andrew's style,
    As high as he could reach.

Grim death, at just that moment micht,*   might
    Hae been old Andra's wush
For the atmosphere resountit
    To a michty empty swush.

His club flew like a rocket
    But, alas, the weird* decreed,   fates
The ba' row'd* two feet sickly   rolled
    An' just lay doon an' died.

Oor John noo steeped forward
    A' een* on him were set,   eyes
An' caddies o' the Skeebo tribe
    Looked dour and glum you bet.

John waggled free and easy like
    As he looked doon at the ba'
But he wisna taking chances
    Wi' old Andra' ava'.*   at all

Sae takin' extra care he drave
    A laich* and rinning ba'.   low
An' Andra' was richt vext tae find
    He'd be on the green in twa.*   two

Auld Andra' took his trusty cleek
    An' fire wis in his ee
Tae try an' make a brilliant shot
    An' lat his backers see

That he wis in the rinnin' still
    An' could the game still win.
By swipin' sic* a mar-vellus shot   such
    An' holling the next yin.

He missed the ba' and brake his club,
    Then kicked it wi' his fit,*   foot
Which pit* him far's the game's concerned   put
    Just hors-de-com-bat.*   beyond hope

Ah, somewhere in this bonnie land
    The pipes skirl* a' the day,   play
An' somewhere lads and lassies shout
    An' men are passing gay.

But they're awfu' dour in Skeebo
    An' nae joy is there aboot,
Sin' the day when, like ane* "Casey,"   one
    Ould Andra' foozled oot.

7th Hole. Parodies

Before you tee off on this hole, here is some home-course advice. You may find the 7th Hole harder to navigate. But if you take your time and keep your "e'e on the ba'," I think you will be rewarded.

In 1901, the American, Henry Walcott Boynton, published a small book of poetry called *The Golfer's Rubaiyat*. It was based on a famous collection of verses called the *Rubaiyat* attributed to the 11th century Persian mathematician and astronomer Omar Khayyam. ("Rubaiyat" is the plural form of "rubai," an Arabic word that defines a rhyme scheme in which the first, second, and fourth lines of each four line stanza rhyme.) During his lifetime, Omar the tentmaker (that's what Khayyam means in Persian), wrote a large number of rubai of a philosophical nature, in addition to his scientific work. In 1859, more than 700 years after Khayyam's death, the English writer Edward FitzGerald published the first translation of some of Omar's verses. He called the resulting poem the *Rubaiyat*. FitzGerald published three more translations in 1868, 1872 and 1879, the longest at 114 stanzas. By the turn of the 20th century, the *Rubaiyat* had become vastly popular both as a poem to read and as a poem to parody.

Henry Boynton, the first golfing poet to parody the *Rubaiyat*, was born in Guilford, Connecticut in 1869 and educated at Amherst College where he earned both a Bachelors and Masters of Arts. He was chief reviewer for *Atlantic Monthly* from 1901 to 1904. He wrote for the *Nation* and the *New York Evening Post* beginning in 1912. He was the author or editor of at least twenty-four books, often using the pseudonym John Walcott. *The Golfer's Rubaiyat* was one of his earliest books. Boynton's publisher, Herbert S. Stone and Company, also published works of George Bernard Shaw putting Boynton, the writer, in good company.

Boynton's *Rubaiyat* parody includes 79 stanzas. Boynton's poetry illuminates his almost mystical understanding of golf. Sadly, though, I could find nothing about his connection to the game other than this one extensive work.

Boynton did not just write a very long golf poem using the *Rubaiyat's* rhyming scheme. Instead, he took certain stanzas from FitzGerald's translations and transposed them to tell a golf-related story in his parody. To give you an idea on how Boynton changed Khayyam's work, compare the fifth stanzas of both poems. First, from the Rubaiyat:

Iram indeed is gone with all his Rose,
And Jamshýd's Sev'n-ring'd Cup where no one knows;
 But still a Ruby gushes from the Vine,
And many a Garden by the Water blows.

Boynton's fifth verse is a little easier to understand:

Campbell indeed is past with all his Fame,
And old Tom Morris now is but a name;
 But many a Jamie by the Bunker blows,
And many a Willie rules us, just the same.

Two of the Jamies to which Boynton refers were the Scottish golfers Jamie Anderson, who won The Open three times and Jamie Braid, who won it five times. Braid was a member of the "Great Triumvirate" along with Harry Vardon and J. H. Taylor.

One of the Willies was Willie Smith. While working as a professional at the Midlothian Country Club near Chicago, he won the 1899 U.S. Open played at the Baltimore Country Club in Maryland. He won by a margin of eleven shots, a record until Tiger Woods won the 2000 championship by fifteen. Smith's prize was $150; Tiger's $800,000! Smith played a total of nine U.S. Opens and made the top ten in eight of them, but he never won again.

Smith became the pro at the Mexico City Country Club in 1904 and was critically injured while hiding in the cellar when Mexican revolutionaries shelled the clubhouse in 1915. The *New York Times* reported that he died in December of 1916 of pneumonia.

Willie Campbell, another Willie and most likely the Campbell referred to in the first line of Boynton's verse, was born in Musselburgh, Scotland in 1862 and died in Boston. He was the first professional at the Country Club in Brookline,

Massachusetts and is credited with establishing the foundations of the present course.

Other Willies include Willie Park, Jr., Willie Auchterlonie, Willie Dunn, Jr., Willie Anderson, Willie Fernie and Willie Davis. This last Willie, when he was appointed the golf professional at Royal Montreal in 1881, became the first golf professional in North America. In 1891, Davis was hired by the founders of the Shinnecock Hills Golf Club to design a twelve-hole course. Willie Dunn, Jr. turned Shinnecock into an eighteen hole course in 1895. Herbert Warren Wind in his book, *The Story of American Golf,* joked that when Willie Dunn, Jr. beat Willie Campbell and Willie Davis in 1894, at what was later considered the unofficial inception of the United States Open Championship, "many Americans deduced that every golf pro had to be named Willie . . . "

Just trying to read those four lines of Khayyam's poem above affirms how difficult the original is to understand. However, the comparison of a few more stanzas proves how cleverly, perceptively and delicately Boynton converted Khayyam's work. The numbers in parenthesis are stanza numbers from FirzGerald's fourth translation, and the Roman numerals refer to Boynton's stanzas.

(27)
Myself when young did eagerly frequent
Doctor and Saint, and heard great Argument
    About it and about: but evermore
Came out by the same Door where in I went.

XXVII
Myself when young did eagerly frequent
Jamie and His, and heard great argument
    Of Grip and Stance and Swing; but evermore
Found at the Exit but a Dollar spent.

(28)
With them the seed of Wisdom did I sow,
And with my own hand wrought to make it grow:
    And this was all the Harvest that I reap'd—
"I came like Water, and like Wind I go."

XXVIII
With them the seed of Wisdom did I sow,
And with mine own hand sought to make it grow;
    And this was all the Harvest that I reap'd—
"You hold it This Way, and you swing it So."

(40)
As then the Tulip for her morning sup
Of Heav'nly Vintage from the soil looks up,
    Do you devoutly do the like, till Heav'n
To Earth invert you—like an empty Cup.

XXXI
As then the Sparrow for his morning Crumb
Do thou each Morrow to the First Tee Come,
    And play thy quiet Round, till crusty Age
Condemn thee to a hopeless Dufferdom.

(71)
The Moving Finger writes; and, having writ,
Moves on: nor all thy Piety nor Wit
    Shall lure it back to cancel half a Line,
Nor all thy Tears wash out a Word of it.

XLVIII
The swinging Brassie strikes; and have struck,
Moves on; nor all your Wit or future Luck
    Shall lure it back to cancel half a Stroke,
Nor from the Card a single Seven pluck.

(63)
Oh threats of Hell and Hopes of Paradise!
One thing at least is certain—This Life flies:
    One thing is certain and the rest is lies;
The Flower that once is blown for ever dies.

XLIX
No hope by Club or Ball to win the Prize;
The batter'd, blacken'd Remade sweetly lies,
    Swept cleanly from the Tee; This is the truth:
Nine-tenths is Skill, and all the rest is Lies.

Golf is surely part skill and part lies, but what about the
mental side? George Duncan and Bernard Darwin in their
book *Present Day Golf* observe, "It is a maxim of Mr. Charles
Hutchings (British Amateur Championship in 1902 when a
grandfather) that 'Golf is nine-tenths mental.'" Thus, between
Boynton and his focus on skill and Hutchings and his focus
on the mental side of the game we end up with a golf Yogi-
ism:

◆ *Golf Is*

The numbers really don't add up
But nevertheless it's true,
Golf is nine-tenth skillfulness
And nine-tenths mental too.

Back to Omar Khayyam and Boynton's parody. One of
the *Rubaiyat's* most famous stanzas is number twelve:

A Book of Verses underneath the Bough,
A Jug of Wine, a Loaf of Bread—and Thou
    Beside me singing in the Wilderness—
Oh, Wilderness were Paradise enow!

In his twelfth stanza, Boynton responds with:

A bag of Clubs, a SilverTown or two,
A Flask of Scotch, a Pipe of Shag—and Thou
    Beside me caddying in the Wilderness—
Ah Wilderness were Paradise enow.

The Silvertown was a brand of golf ball made in the 1880's. Silvertowns were composite balls that flew better and longer than the gutta-percha balls that they replaced.

Below are a few more of Boynton's stanzas that show just how well he understood the game and how he felt about it. If you would like to read *The Golfer's Rubaiyat* in its entirety, visit the Google Books website. Alternatively, a new inexpensive copy of the book has been put out by the Wildhern Press.

LXV
 The Game that can with Logic absolute
 The Dronings of the Soberheads confute,
     Silence the scoffing ones, and in a trice
Life's leaden metal into Gold transmute.

LXVI
Indeed, the brave Game I have loved so well
Has little taught me how to buy or sell;
    Has pawn'd my Greatness for an Hour of Ease,
And barter'd cold Cash for—a Miracle.

LXVII
Indeed, indeed, Repentance oft before
I swore—but it was Winter when I swore,
    And then and then came Spring, and Club-in-hand
I hasten'd forth for one Round—one Round more.

And Boynton's last two stanzas:

LXXVIII

Yon rising Moon that leads us Home again.
How oft hereafter will she wax and wane;
    How oft hereafter rising wait for us
At this same Turning—and for *One* in vain.

LXXVIX

And when, like her, my Golfer, I have been
And am no more above the pleasant Green,
    And you in your mild Journey pass the Hole
I made in One—ah! Pay my Forfeit then!

Surprisingly, Henry Boynton's golfing parody of the *Rubaiyat* is not unique, although it is the most extensive. In searching through old golf books and magazines, I found six more parodies, four of which I reference below! The last was published by an English writer in 1946, forty-five years after Boynton's.

The July 1910 issue of the magazine *The American Golfer* included a poem called "Golfer Omar's Honor." The poet, Jack Warbasse, follows the rhyming form of the *Rubaiyat* and like Boynton bases each of his thirteen stanzas on one of the originals, more or less. To give you a sense of his take on Omar's verses, consider his fifth and thirteenth stanzas:

V. (Related to (33) in FitzGerald 4th Ed)
Myself when young did eagerly frequent
Travis and Braid, and read great argument
    About the Grip and Stance; but evermore
Play'd out by the same Stump where in I went.

XIII. (Related to (101) in FitzGerald 2nd Ed.)
At scratch the Idol I have played so long,
What shall I do, now that my Game's gone wrong?
    I'll drown my glory in the nineteenth cup
And sell my Dreadnought driver for a song.

Neither the poet nor the magazine's editor makes mention of Boynton's earlier work which, as we have seen, is both longer and more cleverly done.

In 1913 a slender book of eighteen pages called *The Rubaiyat of Golfer Guyem* was published in Milwaukee, Wisconsin. This obscure illustrated parody written by Charles H. Moore contains thirty-three stanzas. Today only three copies of the book are accessible, two in university libraries and the other in the Library of Congress.

Moore's verses follow the rhyming scheme of the *Rubaiyat,* but he does not for the most part link his verses closely to stanzas in the original. However, Moore's poem would indicate that he was a golfer with the requisite sense of humor. Consider his verses VI and VII:

Come; fill the glass and from its warmth within,
Fling truthfulness aside and lie like sin
   And tell how on that other course you played,
How, less than bogy [sic] you did make it in.

Whether at Annandale or Babylon,
Pineharst [sic], Fairmont or stately Washington,
   The Highball rare imagination fires,
And Lies of Golf keep coming one by one.

Like the others, Moore parodies Khayyam's verse twenty-seven:

Myself when young did eagerly hang round,
The links, to catch the snappy vigorous sound
   Of talk by Cranks, of Hazard, Bunker, Tee
And mystic terms which did my brain Dumbfound.

Moore's humor turns to feelings of regret and finality in his last stanza:

The song is done; Golf's fleeting Glories pass
Sour words, sweet thoughts alike dissolve in gas
   The game was merry, but too short the while,
The game is finished; turn thou down the glass.

In 1919, a Scottish writer, poet and drama critic, Robert K. Risk, published a book of thirty-six poems under the title *Songs of the Links* with illustration by H. M. Bateman, a famous British cartoonist. The first poem in Risk's collection is "The Golfaiyat of Dufar Hy-Yam," another takeoff on the *Rubaiyat*, this one comprised of seventeen stanzas. Risk, again like the earlier parodists, follows the *Rubaiyat's* rhyming scheme, but he pays only intermittent attention to the text of the original poem. However, his poem reveals the sensibilities of a true St. Andrews' man and lover of the game in the early 20th century. It is worth more than one reading or better, more than one recitation.

◆ *The Golfaiyat of Dufar Hy-Yam*

Awake! for Morning o'er the links of Night
Has driven the Ball that puts the Dark to flight,
   And lo! the Sun has gloriously clad
The Royal and Ancient in a Robe of Light.

Dreaming that I had done a 63,
I heard a Voice exclaim impatiently,
   "Wake up! 'tis nearly half-past Nine O'clock,
There is a Crowd already on the Tee;

And while in drowsy Indolence you snore,
Stentor, the Starter, has been shouting 'Fore!'
   And many a Ball has found the Swilcan-bed,
Many a Man has played the sad Two-More."

So now along the Strip of Herbage strown
With Bunkers, 'twixt the seashore and the sown,
　　We pass, and pity Sultans in their State
To whom the name of Golf is unbeknown.

Here, with an open course from Tee to Tee,
A Partner not too dexterous—like Thee—
　　Beside me swiping o'er Elysian Fields,
And Life is wholly good enough for Me.

"How sweet a well-hit Second Shot!"—think some;
Others—"How true the Putting-Green to come!"
　　Ah! play the Present Stroke, nor heed the Next;
You may adopt that as an Axiom.

The 38 men set their hearts upon
Turns 50—or they prosper; but anon
　　That 79 which seemed a Certainty,
After a Homeward Hole or two—is gone.

Think, in this northern City, old and grey,
Where men talk Golf all night and play all day,
　　How many million Players with their Clubs
Abode a little while, and went their way.

And we who now are topping in the Room
They left, are swiftly passing to the Tomb—
　　Yea, even unto the Grave of Walkinshaw,
For that is our inevitable Doom.

And all the Cracks of yore who once discussed
Of Baffy-Spoons so learnedly, are thrust
　　Like slim Pot-Hunters forth; their words to scorn
Are scattered, and their iron clubs are Rust.

Myself when young did eagerly frequent
Club-makers' Shops, and heard great Argument

Of Grip and Stance and Swing; but evermore
Learned and Bought little I did not repent.

So leave the Cranks to wrangle; and with Me
The Arguments of Theorists let be.
   And softly by the Nineteenth Hole reclined
Make Game of that which maketh Game of Thee.

For out and in, whichever way we go,
Golf is a pleasant kind of Raree-Show
   Full of all sorts of unexpected Fun;
(I would not dare to tell Tom Morris so).

The Ball no question makes of Ayes or Noes,
But right or wrong, as strikes the Player, goes;
   The supercilious Kadi with your clubs
Could tell exactly Why—He knows, He knows!

Ah, Smith, could thou and I with Fate conspire
To grasp this Game in detail and entire,
   And play it perfectly—would we pursue
Our round with greater Relish and Desire?

Dufar Hy-yam! yet keenness knows no wane;
Behold, the Moon has risen once again;
   How oft, hereafter rising, shall she look
Along these self-same Links for Me—in vain!

When Fate has wound me on her direful Reel,
Should Memory ever to your heart reveal
   A thought of Me when you are passing here—
Press down a DIVOT with a pious Heel.

The reference in the ninth stanza is to a local golfer named Walkinshaw who played at St. Andrews. He is described as a player "whose enthusiasm exceeded his proficiency." A pot bunker at the 13th hole from which he often played is named for him, thus "the Gave of Walkinshaw."

In 1946, forty-five years after Herbert Boynton published the first parody, J.A. Hammerton, actually Sir John Alexander Hammerton, a Scottish statesman and author, best-known for his editorship of encyclopedias popular in the first half of the 20th century, published what appears to be the final golfer's *Rubaiyat*, a small book of verses under the title, *The Rubaiyat of a Golfer*. Similar to Boynton, Warbasse, Moore and Risk, each of his four-line verses follows the pattern of the *Rubaiyat* with lines one, two and four rhyming. However, again unlike Boynton's, the verses themselves have relatively few links to Omar Khayyam's originals. In total, Hammerton's book includes thirty-four stanzas, each one illustrated with a cartoon drawn by D.L Ghilchik.

Hammerton's illustrated verses were written with humor and irony. The following will give you an idea of his *Rubaiyat*:

(5)
The "happy medium" is our spirit's quest
Neither to pull nor slice, the one sure test
    As one fault's cured another shows . . . ah, yes,
No Golfer *is*, but always *to be* blest.

(7)
And he who *thinks* he knows how this does that,
Or that does this, is talking through his hat.
    There's No Man knows, though thousands theorize,
And every Pro has explanations pat. ~ ~ ~

(8)
Myself when young would hopefully frequent
Where Pros and Plus Men had great argument
    On Grips that overlapped, on Swing and Stance
But came away less hopeful than I went.

(9)
When "far and sure" I strike from every tee
Does Golfer know a greater ecstasy?
   It's ten to one my Mashie lets me down,
An all my short game will gang clean agley*.   go awry

(20)
And as we lie abed and do the round. . .
In fancy, taking three's and four's, profound
   Is our contempt for those who think we need
As many strokes as shillings to the pound.

(28)
Of all the baleful Partners I have bet
Whose fun'ral would I 'tend with least regret?
   Why his that says when every shot I duff
"Ah, well, we're getting the Fresh Air". . . you bet!

(29)
For I confess, e'en* when I most despair,   even
Let it blow fresh or foul, 'tis *not* the air
   That lures me here, but the wild hope some day
With Braid at the Eighteenth to stand "all square."

(33)
My links are noted for a Lion's Head
A Pit, a Little Hell . . . but be it said
   My favourite is the Churchyard Hole, for there's
My only chance of ever "lying dead."

    The *Rubaiyat* is just one of many famous poems parodied by golfing poets. "The Rime of the Ancient Mariner" is another. Written by the famous English poet Samuel Taylor Coleridge in the years 1797–1799, it begins with the lines,

It is an ancient Mariner,
And he stoppeth one of three.
'By thy long grey beard and glittering eye,
Now wherefore stopp'st thou me?'

Its most famous lines, the last two of which are often misquoted, are,

Water, water, every where,
And all the boards did shrink;
Water, water, every where,
Nor any drop to drink.

Grantland Rice, described by Herbert Warren Wind as "the first important sportswriter who viewed golf as a major sport," used these two stanzas plus the tempo and the rhyming scheme of "The Rime of the Ancient Mariner" in composing his poem "The Rime of the Ancient Golfer."

♦ The Rime of the Ancient Golfer
(Conceding two strokes to Colonel Coleridge)

It was an Ancient Golfer,
  And he stoppeth one of three;
"By thy baffing spoon, thou crazy loon,
  Now wherefore stoppeth me?"

He held me in his glittering eye,
  I had to get that alibi.

"I drove them straight from every tee.
  I soaked them on the crest;
I played my mashie like a Braid,
  Or Vardon at his best.

"But eke when I had reached the green,
  I was a pie-eyed mutt;
I could have had a 68
  If I could only putt.

"I putted slow—I putted fast—
  I made them roll and hop;
I putted standing up and crouched,
  But still they would not drop.

"About—about, in reel and rout,
  My score went on the blink;
Aye, putters, putters everywhere,
  But not a putt would sink.

"I hit the cup eleven times,
  And rimmed it seven more;
Bit my arm, I shrieked aloud,
  I wept and then I swore;

I should have got a 68,
  But got a 94."

I left that crazy loon and ran,
  As any one would do,
And hustled off to tell a guy
  About the putts I blew;

How I deserved a 66,
  And got a 92.

Rice apparently wrote two versions of this poem, the second appearing in his book, *the duffer's handbook of golf*. This version which is longer and follows somewhat closer to Coleridge's original, begins in this manner:

It is an Ancient Duffer
And he stoppeth one of three;
"By that long gray beard and glittering eye,
Now wherefore stoppest thou me?"

And for the "water" verse he has six lines:

"Water, water, everywhere
For every living soul;
Water, water, everywhere
Around the nineteenth hole,
With water hazards on the side
To which my ball would roll."

Overall, however, I think the first version is superior.

In his time, Grantland Rice was referred to as "the dean of American sportswriters." He is most remembered for the awe-inspiring article he wrote about the 1924 Army-Notre Dame football game which began, "Outlined against the blue-gray October sky, the Four Horsemen rode again." The "Four Horsemen" were, of course, the four members of Notre Dame's backfield. Rice is almost universally remembered for the last two lines of a poem called "Alumnus Football":

For when the One Great Scorer comes to write against
    your name,
He marks—not that you won or lost—but how you
    played the game.

"If Gray had been a Golfer" by Samuel E. Kiser, a newspaperman, poet and humorist, parodies another famous poem. Kiser's poem of nine stanzas mimics a much longer poem, "Elegy Written in a Country Churchyard," written by the English poet Thomas Gray and first published in 1751. Gray's poem has been described as "one of the greatest poems in the English language," and as such was often a candidate for parody. Two lines from the poem are frequently quoted and have inspired novel and movie titles: "The paths of glory lead but to the grave" and "Far from the madding crowd's ignoble strife."

One of the themes of Gray's poem, embodied in the stanza below, is that poverty or other barriers prevent many talented people from fully exercising their capabilities.

> Full many a gem of purest ray serene,
> The dark unfathom'd caves of ocean bear:
> Full many a flow'r is born to blush unseen,
> And waste its sweetness on the desert air.

Kiser adopted this theme for his poem by memorializing the "golfless" poor.

"If Gray had been a Golfer" is included in *The Little Book of Sports* published in 1910. Why Kiser, who seemed to be noted for inspirational and humorous poetry, should write such an unusual and somber golf poem is unclear.

♦ *If Gray had been a Golfer*

> Beneath these rugged elms, that maple's shade,
> Where heaves the turf in many a mouldering heap,
> Each in his last eternal bunker laid,
> The rude forefathers of the hamlet sleep.

> Oft to the harvest did their sickle yield,
> Their furrow oft the stubborn glebe has broke—
> Ah, but they had no mashies then to wield,
> They never learned to use the Vardon stroke.

> The poor old souls! They only live to toil,
> To sow and reap and die, at last, obscure;

They never with their niblick tore the soil—
How sad the golfless annals of the poor!

The pomp of power may once have thrilled the souls
Of unenlightened men—today it sinks
Beneath the saving grace of eighteen holes!
The paths of glory lead but to the links.

Perhaps in this neglected spot is laid
Some heart that would have quickened to the game;
Hands that the lovely baffy might have swayed,
To Colonel Bogey's everlasting shame.

Full many a hole was passed by them unseen,
Because no fluttering flag was hoisted there;
Full many a smooth and sacred putting-green
They tore up with the plough, and didn't care.

Some village Taylor, that with dauntless breast
Could whang the flail or swing the heavy maul;
Some mute inglorious Travers here may rest,
Some Harriman who never lost a ball.

Far from the eager foursome's noble strife
They levelled bunkers and they piled the hay,
Content to go uncaddied all through life,
And never were two up and one to play!

No further seek their hardships to disclose,
Nor stand in wonder at their lack of worth;
Here in these bunkers let their dust repose—
They didn't know St. Andrews was on earth.

In the poem Taylor, Travers and Harriman were three
famous golfers around the turn of the 20th century, J. H.

Taylor, Jerome Travers and Herbert H. Harriman. S.E. Kiser knew his golf and golfers.

The reference to "Colonel Bogey" requires a longer explanation. He was so named by an English golfer named Captain Seely Vidal, in the 1890's. The Colonel was created to represent an invisible skilled opponent that you would play at any golf course. Colonel Bogey's score for each hole would equal that made by "the ordinary scratch player, playing not ideally well, but without a single big mistake." Rank amateurs would then play against Colonel Bogey while professionals and the best amateurs would play against par. In those days, par and bogey were the same for most holes, but in a few cases bogey was one stroke more than par. Today, of course, in the U.S., bogey has come to mean one over par at all holes.

8th Hole. Advice

When it comes to giving golf advice, Horace G. Hutchinson heads the list. Hutchinson was the first Englishman to win the British Amateur Championship. He did it twice, in 1886 and again in 1887. He is also the acclaimed author of many golf books, including *Hints on Golf*, published in 1886, the first golf instruction book. In a section called "Advice to Beginners," Hutchinson writes,

> "Now as a learner you . . . must first laboriously build up your style. The head must necessarily be steady, for it is most important that you should keep your eye fixedly on the ball from the moment that the club-head is lifted from the ground until the ball is struck. 'Keep your eye on the ball,' should be your companion text to 'Slow back.'"

Having said that, even Hutchinson can do no better than quote the four-line verse that was included on the "Practice Tee."

'The apple-faced sage with
   His nostrum for all,
'Dinna hurry the swing, keep
   Your e'e on the ball.'

Golfing and Other Poems and Songs, written by John Thomson, is the title of a "dainty little volume" of forty pages published by Wm. Hodge and Co., Glasgow in 1893. Thompson learned to play golf at St. Andrews. He practiced law in Glasgow but often golfed at North Berwick or Gullane. Thomson was said to be "a man of much culture, the soul of any gathering, poetical, musical, or whatever it might be." Thomson's poem, "The Auld Golfer's Advice," is written in "old Scots" which will slow you down. But its message is worth considering in any language:

♦ The Auld Golfer's Advice

Tak' tent, ye blithe billies wha [Take heed you blithe fellows
   who] drive at the ba
And dinna think strength is the hail o't ava; [And do not
   think strength is the whole of it]
A Samson-like fallow may smash thro' the green,
The airt o't's the pairt o't [The art of it's the part of it] whaur
   gowfin' is seen.

Yet it's no in the e'e, the arm, or the leg,
If they work nae as ane ye're no worth a feg; [If
   they work not as one you're not worth a fig]
Like clockwork a' bits o' the body maun gang,*   must go
Then strike her, my hearties, she'll mak' the

richt sang.*   right song

The king o' the body has aye been the
   heid; [always been the head]
If the ruler is bad, but sma' is the speed.
Gin* ye want to be far, and aye to be sure,   If
Forget nae, my lads, to think a' in your pow'r.

A pompous professor aince,* breaking his club,   once
Received frae* his caddie this pertinent snub   from
"For Latin and Greek, sir, ye may hae a heid,
But in playing at gowf it's brains that ye need."

Young anes think driving will win them the Game,
The auld pawky* putter can bring them to shame;   shrewd
Some swear by the iron, or on the cleek lean,
Play weel wi' [Play well with] them a' ere ye
   challenge the green.

In makin' your matches tak' care what ye do,
Weel made, they're half won, is a saying that's true;
Mind this abune a'* as the very best rule—   above all
Ye're no worth a preen* if ye dinna keep cool.   pin

Gang cannily* on, let this not be forgot,   Go carefully
Because then ye have time to study each shot.
The man in a hurry can never dae* weel.   do
He'll heel her, or tap her, then a's to the deil.*   devil

Wi' clavers and havers [With clovers and
   nonsense] ne'er spoil a guid game
Much gabbin' while playing will never bring fame;
When dune, tak' a drap frae the auld tappet
   hen, [old quart of whiskey,]
And then is the time to fecht* battles again.   fight

Gin* ye want to keep young, and no' to be auld   If

That your bluid should be warm instead o' deid cauld,
To be canty and crouse, not dowie and dowf,
   [merry and bold not sad and gloomy,]
Tak' an auld man's advice by learning tae gowf.

I hope you did slow down and take the time to understand John Thomson's admonitions and to sense his love for
the game. This poem is worth reading more than once.

Since I must classify myself as an "Auld Golfer," I took
the opportunity to pen a light-hearted response:

◆ *Growing Aulder*

I found an auld Scottish poem
Its stanzas bright and concise
Play golf to stay young and cheerful
That was "The Auld Golfer's Advice."

In truth playing won't save you
From aging and all that entails
As I keep walking golf's fairways
The scourge of time prevails.

Growing aulder is mostly a downer
Even though I try to keep up
With age my driving gets weaker
  I'm squinting to see the cup.

But what I've lost to father time
I've gained in smarter play
My chipping and putting are better
Which often saves the day.

By relishing golf's lifelong challenge
I've tried to play it smart
But forget the "canty and crouse"

My description—a grouchy auld fart.

Yet one good thing I can tell you
Regarding the battle I'm waging
My handicap is not rising
As fast as I am aging.

With the coming of each New Year
My hope in turning the page
Keep playing well for long enough
To someday shoot my age.

Andrew Lang, the Scots poet included on the 4th Hole, also wrote the following poem full of good golfing advice:

◆ Ballade of the Royal Game of Golf

There are laddies will drive ye a ba'
   To the burn frae* the farthermost tee,   stream from
But ye mauna* think driving is a',   you must not
   Ye may heel her, and send her ajee,*   ajar
Ye may land in the sand or the sea;
   And ye're dune, sir, ye're no worth a preen,*   pin
Tak' the word that an auld man'll gie,*   give
   Tak' aye tent* to be up on the green!   Make sure

The auld folk are crouse, and they craw [are
bold and they boast]
   That their putting is pawky and slee; [shrewd and sly]
In a bunker they're nae gude ava', [not good at all]
   But to girn, and to gar [to grimace and make] the
   sand flee.
And a lassie can putt—ony* she,—   any
   Be she Maggy, or Bessie, or Jean,
But a cleek-shot's the billy* for me,   smart one
   Tak' aye tent to be up on the green!

I hae play'd in the frost and the thaw,
    I hae play'd since the year thirty-three,
I hae play'd in the rain and the snaw,
    And I trust I may play till I dee;
And I tell ye the truth and nae lee,*   not lie
    For I speak o' the thing I hae seen —
Tom Morris, I ken,* will agree —   know
    Tak' aye tent to be up on the green!

ENVOY

Prince, faith you're improving a wee,
    And, Lord, man, they tell me you're keen;*   resolute
Tak' the best o' advice that can be,
    Tak' aye tent to be up on the green!

If you make it on to the green, you may want some help
with your putting. I'm not sure I succeeded in reducing all
putting advice to twelve lines, but here is my attempt:

♦ *When Putting*

Line up and trust when putting
Head still a must when putting

A rhythmic swing
Is just the thing when putting

Get rid of fear
At least be near when putting

All are agreed
The first rule is speed when putting

Consistency
The foremost key when putting

The best advice
Don't think twice when putting.

The real question may be whether to think at all when putting or, more generally, when swinging any club. Here are my thoughts on that subject:

♦ The Futility of Thinking

With golf and sleeping
The more that you think
The odds of succeeding
Are likely to shrink.

Be it sheep in a line
Or the ball at address
Your thoughts only lead to
An increase in stress.

But,

To swing without thinking
Requires that you
Fill your mind up with blanks
It's darn hard to do!

One more advisory, this one focusing on the pre-shot routine:

♦ Pre-Shot Routine

Before you start your driver back to swing
Go through a drill that's sure to help a lot.
This pre-shot set of steps will be the thing
That makes your drive a satisfying shot.

Just stand behind the ball and take a glance.
Look down the fairway taking hazards in.
Select a target, give yourself a chance,
To put your second shot beside the pin.

Now place your driver just behind the ball.
Then aim the club-face at the mark you chose.
Align your feet, remember to stand tall
And swing into a perfect ending pose.

The ball went wide, the bads outweighed the goods.
Well, before the swing you looked like Tiger Woods.

Giving advice is one thing; getting it is another. As the
next poem by Grantland Rice makes clear, for golf at least,
advice from a fellow golfer may not be so welcome:

◆ The Lone Kick

I do not mind the sloping green,
The pits that wind and creep;
I like the bunker's noble mien,
Though heel prints there are deep.

I do not mind the mutt who talks
Just as I swing away,
I do not curse the hick who stalks
In line just as I play.

My temper's soft by green and tee
Though winter winds may blow;
There isn't much that bothers me
No matter where I go.

But where I burn is when some dub
Whose game is none too strong,

Horns in each time I fluff or flub
To tell me what was wrong.

9th Hole. Clerihews

Before making the turn to the back nine, meet E. C. Bentley, an English journalist and novelist whose initials stood for "Edmund Clerihew." He wrote a detective novel called *Trent's Last Case* that was first published in 1913 and later adapted into three movies. In addition, Bentley is the inventor of a particular type of poem that has become known as the "Clerihew." Clerihews are four-line verses where the first two and the last two lines each rhyme. Beyond their rhyming scheme, Clerihews have a particular structure and purpose. Each focuses on one or more aspects of the life and/or works of a famous person while allowing for, or better yet, even encouraging overstatement, distortion and humor. A Clerihew's first line begins or ends with the person's name. When Bentley was sixteen, he wrote his first Clerihew:

> Sir Humphry Davy
> Detested gravy.
> He lived in the odium
> Of having discovered Sodium.

E. C. Bentley may or may not have been a golfer, but he wrote at least two golf Clerihews. The first takes Henry Cotton to task, though a three-time winner of the British Open:

♦ Henry Cotton

One day the putting of Cotton
Was so indescribably rotten
That H. H. [his highness] the Sultan of Johore
Beat him by 6 and 4.

And the second speaks for itself:

♦ Methuselah

In later life Methuselah
Became a hopeless foozler
After he was 765
He practically never hit a decent drive.

Clerihews are definitely fun to write. Here are a few that I penned:

♦ Tiger Woods

About Tiger Woods
It's now understood
To be close to redic'lous
That he won't top Jack Nicklaus.

♦ Byron Nelson

Lord Byron Nelson

To Tiger: "Well, son,
If you want to top my show,
You must win 12 in a row."

✦ Harvey Penick

Harvey Penick
(Rhymes with scenic)
His claim to fame:
"Take dead aim."

✦ Jack Nicklaus

Jack Nicklaus (the Golden Bear)
Pudgy in profile with blondish hair
Left opponents in the dust
With his putting, most robust.

✦ Vardon, Taylor and Braid

Vardon, Taylor and Braid
"The Great Triumvirate" so portrayed
In tournaments, to their competitors' chagrin,
One of the three would usually win.

✦ Vardon and Ray

The Englishmen Vardon and Ray
Golf's best did they convey
But at Brookline their play went astray
As young Ouimet showed them the way.

This last Clerihew refers to the U.S. Open Championship held at The Country Club in Brookline, Massachusetts in September 1913 where Francis Ouimet, a 20 year-old amateur from Brookline, won in an eighteen hole playoff over the British greats Harry Vardon and Ted Ray. The British correspondent to *The American Golfer*, Henry Leach, ended his long and detailed account of the five days of the Open with,

> "I have seen many championships played for in different lands during many years, but I have never seen one better or more thoroughly won than this one. It was a splendid victory most richly deserved . . ."

Though Clerihews are usually about people, they can be about other things as well, as long as the form stays the same.

♦ Slow Play

Slow play
Is no way
To win friends among those
On whom you impose.

When tired of crossword puzzles and Sudokus, you might try writing a golf Clerihew.

10th Hole. Politics and War

Now turning for home, we present stories and poems on this 10th Hole that connect golf with politics or war. The first involves a threat to the 1913 Open Championship from a group of politically charged women.

In England, starting in 1866, a women's movement known as the "suffragists" began working for the vote. In 1903, a violent offshoot of this movement, called the "suffragettes," instituted militant means to force the issue. One of their tactics was to destroy the turf at golf courses. Such a peril was reported in the May 1913 issue of *The American Golfer.*

"... that if they could manage it, the 'wild women,'
as they are being called, meant to do some consider-

able harm to the [Royal Liverpool Club] and inter-
fere as far as they could with the success of what is
expected to be the biggest championship meeting
that has ever taken place."

The article then explains how this threat was met:

". . . in the emergency the club called on the villagers
to assist them in the protection of the course
. . . These efforts were successful and the 1913 Open
Championship went off without any problems."

An unknown poet provided an eight line "remedy" for
this golf course terrorism. The poem appeared in the April
1913 issue of *The American Golfer*.

◆ *The Remedy*

When Suffragettes deface our greens
By various unlawful means,
What shall we golfers do to these
Intolerable Divottees?

Clear is the answer in our rules,
Plain to be read by even fools:
"Replace the turf!" and why not let
It be above the Suffragette?

The St. Andrews poet of the 2nd Hole, George Fullerton
Carnegie, makes clear in the last stanza of his poem, "First
Hole at St. Andrews on a Crowded Day," that politics did not
pass by the first tee at the Old Course in his day.

But when we meet, as here, to play at golf,
Whig, Radical, and Tory—all are off—

Off the contested politics I mean—
And fun and harmony illume the scene.
We make our matches from the love of playing,
Without one loathsome feeling but the *paying*.
And that is lessened by the thought, we *borrow*
Only to-day what we shall *win* to-morrow.
Then, here's prosperity to Golf! and long
May those who play be cheerful, fresh, and strong;
When driving ceases, may we still be able
To play the *shorts, putt*, and be comfortable!
And, to the latest, may we fondly cherish
The thoughts of Golf—so let St. Andrews flourish!

The American woman poet Sarah N. Cleghorn, born in 1876, was a peaceful but committed activist in reform movements ranging from anti-lynching to opposition to child labor. She was probably not a golfer, but, nevertheless, in the January 1, 1915 issue of the *New York Tribune*, she may have written the most arresting four lines of golf-related poetry ever penned:

♦ *The Golf Links*

The golf links lie so near the mill
    That almost every day
The laboring children can look out
    And see the men at play.

This stanza was actually part of a larger work, "Through the Needle's Eye," that was used as part of a campaign to outlaw child labor.

Before going on to poetry related to World War I, I would like to offer a short poem that contrasts golf and politics:

♦ Games People Play

Golf is a game
To be played honestly
But not too seriously.

Politics is a game
To be played seriously
But not too honestly!

Robert Stanley Weir, a Canadian, wrote a poem, "The Plains of Abraham," published in the April 1915 issue of *Golf Illustrated and Outdoor America*. Weir, a Montreal judge, writer and poet, was most famous for writing in 1908 the first English lyrics to *O Canada*, Canada's national anthem. Today's official English lyrics to the anthem are based on Weir's original version. A little digging also shows that Weir was a golfer and frequent contributor to *Golf Illustrated*. He wrote book reviews and several articles on swing mechanics. One titled "Braid or Vardon, Which?" focuses on the swings of these two champions and ends with the thought:

> "Whether we essay the mighty Vardonian sweep or Braid's whip-like, corkscrew-like snap, let us beware of adopting one theory to the denial of any other possible one. It is a great satisfaction and advantage to be able to recognize and adopt both."

Clearly the Judge was a student of the game.

The title of Weir's poem, "The Plains of Abraham," refers to a plateau just outside the wall of Quebec City where a famous battle was fought between the British and French on September 13, 1759. The British won this pivotal battle; however, the British commander, General James Wolfe, was mortally wounded and died on the battle field. The French commander, Louis-Joseph de Montcalm, was also mortally wounded and died the next day. From 1874 to 1915, Cove Fields on the Plains of Abraham was the site of the Quebec Golf Club. This background is needed to understand the setting for the poem. The poem, written at the beginning of the First World War, is a strong and heartfelt statement against war.

♦ The Plains of Abraham

Here, where so long ago the battle roared
Sore frighting Dawn when, trembling, she arose
And saw the precious blood of Wolfe out-poured
And France's hero sinks to long repose.

The grass, they say, is greener for the red
That drenched these plains and hollows all about;
And those thrice fifty years or more have spread
 Much peacefulness on glacis and redoubt. [defensive forti-
fications]

Yes, Mother Nature, grieving, hideth soon
All trace of battles, ravage, death and pain.
The birds began to sing that afternoon—
The dusty, trodden grass to rise again.

And many a year the Citadel's gray walls
Have seen the quiet golfers at their play:
Passing old ramparts, rusted cannon-balls,
And sighting gunless ships the river way.

Thrilled with the peace of golf the players said:
"Those cruel wars can ne'er again have birth;
The living shall no longer mourn their dead
Untimely gathered to reluctant earth."

"The tribes shall rest—nor nearer conflict come
Than when a friendly foursome play the game;
The roaring voice of Wrath is stricken dumb
O better brotherhood than battle-fame!"

But, hark, the roaring of unnumbered guns
By salt Atlantic breezes hither blown!
And bitter cries from countless weeping ones,
While Peace is wringing her cold hands alone!

Rudyard Kipling, the famous English author and poet born in Bombay, India in 1865, was also a golfer. He wrote many famous poems including "Mandalay" and "If . . ." In the following dramatic First World War poem, "Mine Sweepers," he includes a reference to golf. The "Foreland" in the poem probably refers to headlands between Dover and Margate on the southeastern coast of England, overlooking the English Channel.

♦ The Mine-Sweepers

Dawn off the Foreland—the young flood making
Jumbled and short and steep—
Black in the hollows and bright where it's breaking—
Awkward water to sweep.
"Mines reported in the fairway,
"Warn all traffic and detain.
"Sent up Unity, Claribel, Assyrian, Stormcock, and Golden Gain."

Noon off the Foreland—the first ebb making
Lumpy and strong in the bight.
Boom after boom, and the golf-hut shaking
And the jackdaws wild with fright.
"Mines located in the fairway,

"Boats now working up the chain,
"*Sweepers—Unity, Claribel, Assyrian, Stormcock, and Golden Gain.*"

Dusk off the Foreland—the last light going
And the traffic crowding through,
And five damned trawlers with their syreens blowing
Heading the whole review!
"Sweep completed in the fairway,
"No more mines remain.
"*Sent back Unity, Claribel, Assyrian, Stormcock, and Golden Gain.*"

According to Alastair Wilson, a Kipling expert, the "golf-hut" in the second stanza might have been the club-house at Royal St. George's Club at Sandwich, in East Kent.

I found another unusual connection between the First World War and golf poetry in the Foreign Notes section of the March 1917 issue of *The American Golfer*. The British correspondent Henry Leach reported that four of England's greatest golfers were asked to write four-line poems that as a group would be "disposed of in the way of lottery for the benefit of one of the war funds." The four were Harry Vardon, J. H. [John Henry] Taylor, James Braid and Alexander Herd, who beat Vardon and Braid to win the 1902 British Open Championship. The poems were written, framed and delivered to the Mid-Surrey Golf Club where the lottery took place. Leach included all four poems in his report, the first by J. H. Taylor:

Don't lift your head too soon to look
Thinking to see the ball lie "dead."
Such actions sure disasters brook;
Persisted in, *you'll* die instead.

Leach's sympathetic characterization of Taylor's effort: "Rhyme and wit and puns and good solid instruction too." The next is by Harry Vardon:

> He should wear an angel's wings
> Who paths of truth hath trod.
> When left alone with just two things—
> His Score Card and his God.

Leach's initial response is amazement, "This is tremendous. There is hardly anything like it in the whole library and history of poetry." But then he expresses puzzlement:

> "Only, as practical men we wonder why one is less liable to speak or think the truth about one's own score when alone than at any other time, for that seems to be what is meant."

Leach's reaction to Vardon's effort might have extended to the source of this poem. Unless Vardon used the pen-name Douglas Malloch, he must have taken the lines from the fourth stanza of Malloch's poem called "Golf" that appeared in the September 1912 issue of *American Golfer*, four and a half years earlier.

> It is a game of honor, too,
>   That tries the souls of men.
> It's easy in the public view
>   To all be honest then;
> But he deserves an angel's wings
>   Who paths of truth has trod
> When left alone with just two things—
>   His score card and his God.

What is more likely is that Vardon, who quit school at the age of 12, asked one of his more literate friends to supply him with the needed four lines. The friend came across Malloch's poem and gave Harry the four lines with minor changes from the original.

James Braid used his four lines as a simple disclaimer:
A golfer humble I hope I am,
And trust that others know it;
But unlike my confreres who can rhyme
I surely am no poet.

Finally, we have the Alexander Herd's contribution:

It gladdens the heart and it lightens the brain
To chase the wee ball and then loft it again.
There's health on the moor, on the sands, on the hill
Surpassing the time of potion or pill.

As Leach concludes, "It has been a pleasant interlude with these poets." He did not report on whether the lottery had any takers!

Henry Leach began writing on the impact of the First World War in his Foreign Notes section almost from the moment war began. Britain declared war on Germany on August 4, 1914. Leach, in a ten-page report dated September 1, 1914, focuses almost entirely on the war and its impact on golf in England. Right from the beginning, he shows how personal the war has become to him:

"The boy who has been in the habit of most frequently carrying my clubs for me on my favourite links has enlisted in the army and is now fighting for the safety of his country like hundreds of other caddies have done."

Two months later, Leach includes in his column a resolution issued by one of the London area golf clubs and typical of others sent out by "practically every club of importance."

> "Dear Sir—I am instructed by the committee to send a copy of the following resolution, passed by the committee, to every member of the club: Resolved, that a circular be issued by the secretary to all members of the club, suggesting that during the continuance of the present war, it would be an act of delicacy and avoid the possibility of situations of embarrassment if those members who are of German or Austro-Hungarian origin, whether naturalised or not, should not frequent the club; while all members are requested to refrain from offering hospitality in the club to persons of such origin."

As the war continued, Leach reported its effect on the golf scene month after month. In one column he talks of the numbers of club members who have joined the fighting (e. g., 117 from Royal Liverpool, 91 from Royal St. George's). In many columns he chronicles the heroism of noted golfers who were wounded or killed. Late in 1915, he even describes the situation in a prison camp in Germany where "there is more golf being played . . . than anywhere else except in America . . ."

A few months after the war ended, Leach told one more story:

> "Shortly after the British forces occupied Bagdad [sic], a course was laid out and when it was completed thoughts were soon turned to contemplation of the first golf championship of Bagdad. A competition was duly organized, and the news of it spread

for miles and miles over the surrounding country where the British golfers were, and it is related that one of them, Hardman his name . . . heard of it and that a silver cup was being given for the first prize."

Hardman was a gunner stationed far away from Baghdad, and he had to travel three full days to get there.

"However, he duly reached [the course], teed up in the competition, and achieved his heart's delight, for he won with a score of seventy."

Leach ends the story with, "Such is a little romance of the war and golf."

11th Hole. Links with the Devil

The Faust of classic German legend was not a golfer, but his idea of making a pact with the devil has occurred to golfing poets and, most surely, to golfers having a bad day. Bert Leston Taylor envisages such a golfer in his poem "The Devil's Disciple." Taylor was a newspaper columnist, poet and writer. From 1910, until his death in 1921, he wrote a daily column in the *Chicago Tribune* under the byline "A Line o' Type or Two." During this time he became one of the most widely read newspaper humorists.

Taylor loved golf and was a close friend of Charles "Chick" Evans, Jr., the great American amateur and "chronic semi-finalist." Evans wrote the introduction to *A Line o' Gowf or Two,* a posthumous compilation of Taylor's golf writings and poetry, which includes "The Devil's Disciple." The poem originally appeared in the April 1917 issue of *The American Golfer.*

"The Devil's Disciple" is about a frustrated golfer named "Mac" who reveals his Faustian leanings eight lines into the poem:

> "I never shall learn this game," quoth he.
> "And I'd sell my soul for a seventy-three!"

The poem continues:

> No sooner said, on this fatal night,
> Than the Devil walked in, with a bow polite.
> "Pledge me your soul, my friend," said he,
> "And to-morrow you'll shoot a seventy-three.
>   Don't think at all
>   Of stance or grip;
>   Just swat the ball,
>   And let 'er rip.
> Leave it to me, I'll turn the trick;
> *You* pin your faith to your Uncle Nick."
> "Done!" said the Golfer—"gladly, too."
> "You're on," said the Devil. "Good-night to you."

And, when Mac follows the Devil's advice:

> Next day, when "Mac" drove off the tee
> For the first long hole, he was down in three;
> And every other, or near or far,
> Was played, somehow, in exactly par.

For the entire round, Mac would,

Drive and iron, and pitch and poke,
Till, matching his card, his friends went broke.
For, adding his score, they found that he
Had shot the course in a *seventy-three*.

In considering "Mac's" deal with the Devil, Taylor ends the poem with this observation:

He never worries about the trade,
    Or ever gives it a thought at all:
And the only sign of the pact he made
    Is a puff of smoke where he hits the ball.

Newman Levy was a New York City Assistant District Attorney, a trial lawyer, an opera buff and a writer of light verse. In addition, he wrote for the *New Yorker* and *The Saturday Evening Post* and published several books. I'm pretty sure that in spite of his busy professional life he also found time to play golf. In a ballad called "Told at the Nineteenth Hole," from *Gay But Wistful*, published in 1925, Levy tells the story of Lysander James Adolphus Brown, "the rankest dub," and his link with the Devil.

♦ Told at the Nineteenth Hole

Of all the golfers playing at the Fairgreen Country Club,
Lysander James Adolphus Brown was quite the rankest dub.
His stance was queer, his driving wild, his mashie shots were
    jokes.
The best hole that he ever made took twenty-seven strokes.
At times he'd swing for half an hour and never touch the ball.
It really was a wonder that he tried to play at all.

Now one day when Lysander had been rather off his game,
Into the locker room a handsome, well-dressed stranger came.

His clubs were swung across his back, and as he entered there
A pungent sulphur odor seemed to permeate the air.
He sat down by Lysander, and with just the slightest sneer
He said: "I've watched you play around. You certainly shoot
    queer."
Lysander had a biting wit, as all his club mates knew,
And so he answered like a flash: "Well, what is that to you?"
The stranger smiled and said: "I heard you say you'd sell your
    soul
If you could make a decent score, or even win a hole.
I'm just the man you're looking for. I've got a set of clubs,
Their owner can make Sarazen or Hagen look like dubs.
They're guaranteed, and good as new. I've used them only
    twice."
Lysander James Adolphus Brown said hoarsely: "What's your
    price?"
The stranger's face grew stern, and from his coat he drew a scroll.
"Just sign this and the clubs are yours. The price I ask—your
    soul!"
"There's no mistake," Lysander cried, "and they'll improve
    my game?"
"They're guaranteed," the stranger said.
                           Lysander signed his name.
A smell of brimstone filled the room; then came a thunderclap,
And there Lysander sat, alone. The clubs lay in his lap.

'Twas on the morning of the match, and brightly shone the sun,
And as Lysander reached the tee the crowd said: "Watch the
    fun."
"You laugh too soon," Lysander said. "I'll show you duffers up,
For by to-night my name will be engraven on the cup."
He placed a shiny, brand-new ball upon a mound of sand,
And from his bag he calmly seized his driver in his hand.
A laugh rose from the gallery, but it changed into a shout
When, with a graceful, easy swing, he hit the ball a clout.
It shot right down the fairway like a bullet from a gun.
"It's in the cup!" the gallery cried. "He's made the first in one!

Well, even duffers have their lucky shots," they said, perplexed.
Lysander merely smiled and said: "Just watch me on the next."
The second hole was very long—six hundred yards or more—
And thirty-five or forty was Lysander's average score.
Once more he drove with all his might. The ball sped toward the
    goal.
It landed square upon the green and trickled in the hole.
Then Brown said to his caddy as his ball again he teed:
"Just take that bag back to the club. My driver's all I need."
The crowd no longer ridiculed Lysander's awkward stance,
They followed him around the course like people in a trance,
Until a mighty cheer went up upon the final green.
Lysander nonchalantly said: "That gives me an eighteen."

Then once again the pungent smell of sulphur filled the air,
And turning round, Lysander saw the stranger standing there.
A sudden hush spread o'er the crowd, a stillness filled the place.
A smile of rare contentment gleamed upon Lysander's face.
And the gallery heard him mutter as he took the stranger's hand:
"Well, anyway I guess I made a record that will stand."

John Thomson, the Scottish author and golfing poet we
first met on the 8th Hole, wrote a second short book, this one
thirty-five pages long, called *A Golfing Idyll,* and subtitled, *The
Skipper's Round with the Deil On the Links of St Andrews.* The
book was first published privately in 1892. The Skipper's story
is told in verse composed by Thomson using the pseudonym
"Violet Flint."

In the book's Preface we learn that Flint is a "lady medi-
cal student" on autumn holiday in St. Andrews. She tells us
that one day while sitting on a hill behind the Club House
with "sketch-book in hand," she noticed an "old Caddie" near
by. She describes him as not very creditable, being a sad
victim "of the vice [alcohol] that has cut off so many poor
fellows of his class." But, surprisingly, he is "neatly dressed in

blue serge, a bit of blue ribbon apparent on the lapel of his coat." He is soon joined by another man "who proved also to be a Caddie." Shortly thereafter, the first caddie, "the Skipper," begins to tell his story. Flint remarks upon his discourse:

"Throughout the narrative he was exceedingly animated—rising, sitting down, and gesticulating, as if under the influence of considerable excitement and emotion, evidently earnestly intent on impressing on the listener the truth of what he was relating."

Listening to his story, Flint concludes that the Skipper is better educated than she thought, especially with regard to great literature dealing with the devil and temptation: he refers at one point to John Bunyan of *Pilgrim's Progress*; at another he indicates some acquaintance with John Milton of *Paradise Lost*. When her holiday ended, she returned to London and "most carefully" wrote down what she remembered. She even returned to interview "the old gentleman" several times. Her preface concludes:

"As to my reason for weaving the story into rhyming doggerel, I hold myself excused in that I did it for my own amusement, influenced also by a belief that it might possibly prove more readable and attractive in that shape to the persons I chiefly wish to peruse it, viz., my friends of the Caddie fraternity."

A third edition of *A Golfing Idyll* was published in 1897 in which a few colorful illustrations were added and, somewhat mysteriously (since Thomson died in 1893), an additional preface. We learn from this preface that the Skipper has died "at the ripe old age of 75" and that in Flint's final interview with him, he "pathetically deplored the unreasoning and obstinate incredulity of friends who persisted in disbelieving his story."

I wish that I could include Flint's telling of the Skipper's story in full, but it's too long. Therefore, I will summarize it, including enough lines to convey the spirit of the tale. (The full text can be found on the Internet using Google.)

The poem begins with a description of Jock Pitbladdie, the caddie friend to whom the Skipper tells his story:

A golfer good, and decent caddie
Who, drunk or sober, in's* vocation   in his
Had aye the grace o'moderation
A souter* to his trade, he'd left the toun*   shoemaker town
Sax months before to work in Troon
To carry clubs or mend auld shoon*   shoes
At ilka* trade a handy loon.   every

Pitbladdie looks at the Skipper, dressed so well, and asks how he accomplished his conversion:

No six months gane, a drucken devil,
You led the ball in waste and revel;
Were staggerin' on destruction's brink,
Selling your very duds for drink.

Jock goes on:

Weel washed, weel clad, your blue beard shaved
Like Dr Byd's, and weel behaved
As toun-kirk* elder 'fore the session—   town church
Speak out, auld man, and mak' confession.

The Skipper responds:

Come here, you jawing gowk,* sit doon.   fool
Instead of coorse and ill reflections
On my past life, and ways, and actions,
Your greetin' might hae been more ceevil,
You ill-condeetioned gabbin' deevil.

And then he continues:

Oh, Jock! I doot* I'm rash to tell ye   fear
What strange and awfu' things befell me.

And, thus, the Skipper begins his fantastical story.
    On a summer's afternoon just after Jock had gone to
Troon, the Skipper met up with an "auld mate" named
Tammas Trail from Crail.

A very decent chappie Tam,
Who, like me, dearly lo'ed his dram.*   a small drink of liquor

    They go to supper where the food is hot and good and
the whiskey even better. The merriment ends around ten
o'clock. The Skipper claims that he isn't drunk – "just fresh
and free and swaggerin' canty [cheerfully]." Then he gets an
idea. He would grab his clubs and go to the Links. And when
he arrives, he starts out by himself.

Nigh the brig* I drove a bonny shot,   Near the bridge
My second was the marrow o't*   was the equal of it
The third gaed* in—I holed in three   went
As proud as Punch, I skirled* wi' glee;   shouted

    Happy with his start, he yells, "I'd play the very Deil
[Devil] himsel'." Right then he hears a laugh and turning sees
someone standing nearby.

A strappin' chiel,* wi' clubs in han',—	fellow
Lean-shankit,* extra tall and spare,	Lean-legged
Wi' goatee beard and jet-black hair.	

'Good evening, Skipper,' says he sprightly,
Liftin' his cap to me politely.
'You want a match, I'll gladly play you
For a hundred pounds, what say you?'

The Skipper wants to take the bet but confesses that he is just a poor caddie and never bets more than a shilling. The fellow counters that the Skipper is a "strong, well-known professional" and that he is but a first-class amateur who plays poorly. The fellow continues:

But if you're shy, why odds I'll give you,
A stroke a hole, will that not tempt you?
And should I have the luck to win
(He said this with a leering grin),
Why what so simple, you engage
To serve me faithful without wage,
And as my Caddie with me stay
Until your little debt you pay.

The fellow then shows the Skipper a purse full of "golden guineas," and the Skipper then laments his alcohol-induced decision to Pitbladdie:

Dazed, dazzled, fou,* and half-demented	drunk
Oh, Jocky! I was sairly tempted.	
No wonder that I soon consented,	
And muckle* less that I repented.	much

And so the Skipper takes the bet. He then goes on to describe his opponent in more detail.

His dress was black, good velveteen,
His stockin's red and cravit green,
And on his feet were yellow boots,—
I little dreamed they covered cloots!*   cloven feet

After ending his description, the Skipper continues,

"And what's your honour's name, quoth I?
I felt no whit abased or shy—
"My name is Dr. Nicholas Ben Clootie,
Hades my home, a place of radiant beauty;
A region warm, perhaps a trifle sooty,
Still an alluring and delicious place is Hades,
Frequented much by lords and ladies.

The Skipper and the Devil begin their match on the second hole. When they reach the fifth hole the Skipper is three
up. At this point the Skipper again hits a perfect drive, but the
Devil misses his.

At 'Hole Across,' the bunker of H—l,
To my surprise he kent it well;
He girned* and cackled and looked excited   snarled
As if wi' secret thoughts delighted.
I drove it weel o'er with grand precision
And lay serene on sod Elysian.
Clootie on purpose missed his ba',
And landed slap intil its maw.*   inside its mouth
Then, Jock, a sicht* I saw,   sight
    so strange and awfie,*   shocking
Unseen, unheard o', and unlawfie!
Loud laughter rose from H—l within,
Wild shouts and cries o' welcomin';
While over the edge, peepin' and peerin'
Through the long grass, and disappearin'
Were seen strange forms, like horned apes,

And other brutes wi' fearsome shapes . . .

As they approach the bunker, all that remained was an "infernal smell," the Devil's "favorite scent." Regardless, the Skipper takes the hole and continues to win the next four as well. So after eight holes, he is eight up and needs only one more to win the match. Still, at the turn, the Skipper has not understood who his opponent is.

And my opponent was the Devil.
Blind, stupid, and wi' drink demented,
I could not see nor comprehend it;

Nevertheless, the Skipper is so close to victory that he decides to up the ante saying, "Throw up the sponge, play double or quits!" The Devil responds by calling his bluff and then disappears temporarily.

Gone like a flash, I looked and wondered,
And as I gaped and gazed and pondered,
Beneath my feet the ground began to tremble,
With earthquake shock to rock and rumble;
And o'er the scene thick darkness crept,
Deep gloom prevailed, the soft wind slept,
Then lightning flared with vivid sheen,
Blinding and dazzling my bewildered een!*   eyes

With all the commotion, the Skipper passes out and when he wakes up he feels the soft morning air. His story resumes.

Conscious at last, I raised my eyes,
Conceived my horror and surprise,
To see friend Clootie stand before me,
Leering and grinning, bending o'er me!
My heart was well-nigh like to burst

With fear and hatred and disgust.
I cried, beseeched him to forgive me,
And begged him on my knees to leave me.
He laughed, and told me hold my jargon,
To stir my stumps, make good my bargain.
'The match you know,' he said, 'ain't ended,
And luck may turn, and mine be mended,
The remaining holes may fall to me,
Then Skipper dear, where will you be?
I've not had one, and eight you've taken,
You need one more to save your bacon—
One little hole, to save your soul!

When the Skipper looks at him closely, he sees a trans-
formed person. Then the Devil explains the change:

"To honour you I've changed my suit,
My taste and style none can dispute;
I now assume my sporting dress,
The garb I wear when I mean business;
I've donned my tail, and doffed my boots,
You see me in my native cloots."
Man's fond, familiar, friendly devil
Aye gracious, debonair and civil;
Smiling he stood, his arms akimbo,
The Deil himself, the Prince o'Limbo.

The Skipper, now understanding his dire circumstances,
turns to Heaven to save his soul.

I prayed, as ne'er I prayed before;
In anguish keen I vowed and swore,
This trouble gone, this sorrow ended,
My wicked life should be amended;
This struggle o'er, this combat passed,
This drucken bout should be my last.

Then hope, sweet hope, began to flow,
And swell my breast with genial glow;
Self-trust and courage that had gane*   gone
Wi' fiery rush, cam' back again.
My native pride, love o' the game,
Blazed in my heart like altar flame.
I felt that tho' a fool I'd been,
I still could battle for the green.

The game resumes, but now the Devil is in command.
The Skipper rues his predicament:

I played my best, I strove and swat:
Wha* could contend 'gainst foe like that?   Who
A stroke a hole, what use to me
Against a Deil who averaged three?

Not surprisingly, the next eight holes go to the Devil and
they arrive at the eighteenth all square. Now the Devil speaks:

'Skipper,' quoth he, 'how dost thou feel?
You've had your tussle with the Deil;
Hast got a lesson, eh, in Golf?
Just one hole more and then—enough!
I've seen your swagger, heard your boast,
Methinks I've got you now—on toast.'

The Skipper responds, raising the question as to why he
was chosen and not someone of greater merit.

But michty strange it seems to be,
Sic* honour should be kept for me,   Such
When you might have made selection
From swells and sinners o' distinction:
Ginerals, Cornels, and sodger* gentry;   soldier
Gude kens!* there's wale o' them and plenty!   God knows

'Mong Clairgy, Lawyers, and Professors,
Poor folk in trade, and sma' transgressors.
Save us man! You mich hae grippet
A Provost wi' an ermine tippet,
Or eke a consequential Bailie,*   magistrate
Or Councillor fu' wise and wily.
Instead to nab a poor auld caddie,
'Twas *mean*, I tell't him, Jock Pitbladdie.

The Devil ignores the question and tees off on eighteen.

He drove a long, low ripping shot,
O'er brig and road to the green he got.
I followed true, for me right good,
But, alas, I landed on the road!
My heart it sank, but I lay clean,
For muckle waur* I might hae been.   For a lot worse
I took my cleek—Oh, blessed happy lick!
Home went the ball fornent* the stick   before
Dead as a corp, or Julius Caesar
Balaam's ass, or Nebuchadnezzar.
Forward I ran, richt eager, to the green
To see how good my luck had been.
Fortune indeed had smiled upon me,
I lay a dead and perfect stymie!
Auld Sin he looked as black as thunder
To be so foiled, I dinna wonder.
I sprang wi' glee, and gied* a howl,—   gave
'I've stymed the Deil and saved my sowl!'
'Villain!' he roared, 'You sot, you've done me,
My malison and curse be on ye!
With that he struck me wi' his tail
Right on the stern, just like a flail,
So cruel, strong, severe a lounder,*   beating
In faith it felled me flat's a flounder.

Thus the match ends, but not the poem. What remains is for Violet Flint to expose the poor Skipper for the liar he is. She does, but lets him down easy. He is taken home where "Nurse Killiegrew" and several assistants watch over him for seven days until he "found [his] head." At that point the Skipper tells all to his six women caretakers.

My yarn, of course, made great sensation;
They groaned and grat* at the narration,   cried
Save Nurse, who shook her head in sadness,
Incredulous, declared my story madness.
Said she, 'You fancy you have seen the Deevil,
And golfed and bargained wi' the Prince o' Evil;
You've had the horrors, it would seem,
And what you tell us was a drunkard's dream.'

Though he fails to convince the Nurse, he is indebted to her and ready to reform. The poem ends with the Skipper's redemption:

Gone, gone forever, all the filth and folly,
The aches, the woes, the melancholy;
I've cast the old, put on the new,
Three cheers then for the ribbon blue,
And blessings on Nurse Killiegrew!

The blue ribbon on the Skipper's suit that Violet Flint had noted in her introduction was the badge of a teetotaler in Victorian times.

12th Hole. Mysteries of the Links

TUTOR. "The secret of good putting is never to lift your head until you hear the ball rattle in the tin."
PUPIL. "That's silly. You can't keep gazing at the ground for the rest of your life."

Wallace Stevens, a major American modernist poet, was born in 1879 and lived through the first half of the 20th century. He was renowned for his philosophic poetry that examined the relationship between an individual's thoughts and feelings and the surrounding environment. One of his many poems was titled "Thirteen Ways of Looking at a Blackbird." Using this poem as a starting point for its format and introspection, I have tried to explore the mysteries of putting.

♦ Thirteen Ways of Looking at a Putt
(With apologies to Wallace Stevens)

I
Among the hills and valleys of the green
The only objects moving
Were the eyes of the golfer
Surveying his putt.

II
He was of more than one mind
Like the just finished foursome
Now in the clubhouse bar.

III
Standing behind the ball looking
For the line, he then crouched
For a second look
Reading from his putting book.

IV
A golfer and his putter
Are one
But a golfer and his putter and his putt
Are one
Only if the ball goes in.

V
I do not know which to prefer
The beauty of a perfectly struck putt
Or the beauty of a green at sunset
The ball dropping
Or just after.

VI
The golfer moved around

Behind the pin,
The shadow of a blackbird
Crossing his own shadow
As he took up a new position
From which to trace a path
Ball to hole.

VII
Fellow golfer
Why do you imagine a birdie?
Don't you see the
Difficulties of the putt?
Par is always a good score.

VIII
I know of noble efforts
And of rhythmic swings
But I know too
Not to include all that I know
In preparing for my next putt.

IX
When the ball stopped on the green
It only crossed over the edge
Of the larger circle.

X
At the sight of an unputtable ball
Mired in tall grass beyond a green
The errant golfer
Would like to cry out sharply
And often does.

XI
He rides from green to green
In a golf cart
Often fearful that

What putting skills he has
Will disappear along the path
Between holes.

XII
The putt is rolling off line
His head must have moved.

XIII
Look at a putt thirteen ways,
And you can still miss it.
Or with a quick look
It might go in.

As we have seen on the 4th Hole and we know from our own experiences, the agonies and frustrations of golf are endless. Even the professionals have their daily struggles. Hogan once said, "This is a game of misses. The guy who misses the best is going to win." All of this led me to think about what it would be like to play golf without error.

♦ Perfect Golf

If . . .
in every game all greens were hit
and each was then one putted
would golf as a game
still be the same
its mystery all but gutted?

Errorless play may be the goal
but when you come down to it
to play the best
would end the test
so . . .
would you want to do it?

Robert K Risk, whose poetry appeared on the 7th Hole, gave an answer to my poem, many years before I wrote it, in the last stanza of a poem he called "The Golfer's Discontent."

> And, therefore in a future state
>   When we shall all putt out in two,
> When drives are all hole-high and straight,
>   And every yarn we tell is true,
> Golf will be wearisome and flat,
> When there is naught to grumble at.

W. Hastings Webling, whose poetry is featured on the 19th Hole, published a poem called "Retrospection" in 1915 that also included a stanza with thoughts about perfect golf.

> My boy! If skies were ever fair,
>   If winds should always favor you,
> And all your "lies" were perfect "lies,"
>   And all your putts were straight and true—
> If all your drives were far and sure,
>   Approaches on the green were "dead,"
> The joy of combat would be lost,
>   And vict'ry's charm forever shed.

The mysteries of golf extend also to the inconsistency of play from day to day. Holes played well one day are often played poorly the next for no apparent reason. Edgar A. Guest, the *Detroit Free Press* columnist who once described himself as "a newspaper man who wrote verses," wrote these about golf's "Yesterday."

♦ Yesterday

I've trod the links with many a man,
And played him club for club;

'Tis scarce a year since I began
And I am still a dub.
But this I've noticed as we strayed
Along the bunkered way,
No one with me has ever played
As he did yesterday.

It makes no difference what the drive,
Together as we walk,
Till we up to the ball arrive,
I get the same old talk:
"To-day there's something wrong with me,
Just what I cannot say.
Would you believe I got a three
For this hole—yesterday?"

I see them top and slice a shot,
And fail to follow through,
And with their brassies plough the lot,
The very way I do.
To six and seven their figures run,
And then they sadly say:
"I neither dubbed nor foozled one
When I played—yesterday!"

I have no yesterdays to count,
No good work to recall;
Each morning sees hope proudly mount,
Each evening sees it fall.
And in the locker room at night,
When men discuss their play,
I hear them and I wish I might
Have seen them—yesterday.

Oh, dear old yesterday! What store
Of joys for men you hold!
I'm sure there is no day that's more

Remembered or extolled.
I'm off my task myself a bit,
My mind has run astray;
I think, perhaps, I should have writ
These verses—yesterday.

Golf in its earliest day was played over grounds that were described as "links" when in close proximity to the sea and with few if any trees. However, the links of golf are not limited to literal course descriptions. Mysterious links also exist between golfers of the past, present and future.

◆ Links

Who walks with me
On fresh new-mown grass
Away from the tee
And toward the green?

Sure, I'm in good company
With my three golfing pals
Out early this Sunday.
But what of the others?

Walking in the Scotch-like mist
I sense those hardy souls who played
With mashies, cleeks and feathery balls,
Yet swung with the same hopes and fears.

And what of those right now on other fairways?
Should they not be included as well?
Though all fairways are different,
The walk we share is the same.

And what of you who follow in my footsteps?
As I feel your presence now

So might you imagine an echo
As your shoes fill-in for mine.

Across these fairways of time and space
Golfers share a sacred link.
Our places secure in a continuing march
Watched over by the gods of golf.

This reverence for the game
So familiar to us all,
Is passed from generation to generation
On the paths we follow from tee to green.

13th Hole. Golf Dreams

THE GOLFER'S DREAM

The next best thing to playing golf just might be dreaming about playing golf. Particularly, since when we are dreaming, we seem to have much better control over everything including our swings and scores. Furthermore, we have no need to ask for the Devil's help. John Thomson, whose poem "The Golfing Idyll" we just read at the 11th Hole, amusingly described this approach to perfect golf:

♦ Perfection

Oh! I played at golf once on a beautiful day,
O'er a green round the marge of a wide sweeping bay,
Where the sea lay in calm, like a babe when at rest,
In a sweet dreamless sleep on a fond mother's breast.

This course it was perfect, for both Nature and Art
Had vied with each other which would best do her part,
And the game that I played—well, the like was ne'er seen
By the eye of a mortal before on a green.

Holes in one were quite common, the longest in two;
Aye, all this, in plain truth, I could easily do;
Yet a pro at his best, with a card at his back,
Would find it hard work a poor eighty to crack.

Now, professional golfers with envy may groan,
And that they are nowhere must candidly own,
Or my card, rightly kept, came to not a stroke more
Than, when properly added, made up twenty-four.

There the golfers could count well, and knew the strict rules,
Nor went writing about them like so many fools;
No player e'er thought mean advantage to take,
But played as if honour alone were at stake.

There the caddies were civil, and sober, and clean,
Were all sturdy, well clad, not one ragged or lean;
If you offered them money, they looked in despair,
And would carry your clubs for the sake of the air.

The club-makers trusty kept well-seasoned wood,
The best to beginners they gave of the good;
The balls that they sold were sound as a bell,
With both paint and weight right, not made merely to sell.

The green-keepers wrought hard when no one was nigh,
And never sat down for some hours on the sly,
Or went dodging or cringing, with bow and with beck,
While just leaving the course to sheer ruin and wreck.

Many far-away friends did I meet on that green,
Kind faces for years I had never once seen;
E'en dead golfers were there, all quite pleasant and gay,
Appeared to be living, so keen did they play.

Quick as lightning's bright flash on the bosom of night,
All, all in a moment was lost to my sight,
A voice yelled, "Get up"! It was cruel, I deem,
To be rudely awakened from such a fine dream.

The last stanza of the next poem assures it a place in this
hole of reveries.

♦ When Golf Is the Game

When golf is the game
And skill is the claim
You have no excuses
For golf club misuses.

When golf is the game
Take care where you aim
If a shot goes awry
There's no second try.

When golf is the game
None else is to blame
See water when set
Your ball ends up wet.

When golf is the game
It seems quite a shame
To pay a big fee
Then shoot 103.

When golf is the game
True links-men can name
The reasons they play
Without shades of grey.

When golf is the game
Every dream is the same
All is at stake
Just when you wake.

The next poem is by Ring W. Lardner, the famous American humorist, sports columnist and master short story writer. It appeared originally in his column in the *Chicago Tribune* and was reprinted in the September 1918 issue of *The American Golfer*. He also played well horizontally.

♦ Nocturnal Golf

I played a wonderful game— for me—
    And found, when I'd got all through,
That I'd cut my score to a 43
    From my usual 62.

On the first, which commonly takes me an 8,
    Because I am not warmed up,
My drive and brassey were long and straight,
    And my fifth dropped into the cup.

On the second, where I so often dub,
    With both of my wooden sticks,
I was there like a duck with either club

And holed in a bogey 6.

On the third, where one of the apple trees
    Habitually stops my drive,
I missed the fruit with the greatest ease
    And was down in a nice par 5.

I shunned both hazards on No. 4,
    The bois* and the deep ravine,   woods
And trimmed two strokes from my normal score
    By mashieing to the green.

On the fifth, where I frequently take a dip
    Or two in the seething foam,
Two aerial swats and a mashie chip
    Were plenty to bring me home.

On the sixth, where my second is wont to seek
    A nest in the tall uncut,
I stopped at the edge with my third, a cleek
    And was in with my second putt.

On the seventh—(they call it a mashie pitch,
    And Lord how you've got to soar!)
I flew high over the hellish ditch
    And was down in a couple more.

On the eighth—it's one of those tricky holes,
    And a 6 is my common lot—
I cleared the cunning but nasty knolls
    With a beautiful midiron shot.

On the ninth, where in every unfriendly match
    I chum with the Horti Cult,
I scorned Mrs. Wiggs and her cabbage patch,
    And a 6 was the result.

I made the nine in a 43
    Last night, as I lay in bed.
Oh, golf is no trouble at all for me
    When I play a round in my head.

The credit for the next ode to bedtime golf goes to H.T. Watkins, who served as the chairman of the green committee of the Meadow Brook golf course in Reading, Massachusetts when the poem was published. It appeared without a title in *The American Golfer* in March 1914.

My good scores come to me in dreams.
In spite of all, to me it seems
No matter how I try, and try,
I can't play good golf if I die.

I've played the game for ten long years;
I've chased the pill with oaths, and tears;
I've seen a good score just ahead,
But never made it,—save in bed.

Like all the other golfing fools,
I buy a bag of shining tools;
I take them out upon the course
And use them like a foundered horse.

I schlaffe and foozle, slice and hook,
Dig up the turf, get in the brook;
But when at eve I seek repose
Such scores I make nobody knows.

When night comes on, I lay my head
In peace upon my downy bed
And pound my ear; and all the while
I dream I belt the ball a mile.

And grab my mashie by the neck
And then hole out in two, by heck.
Each hole in par I seem to make,
Mark down my score, and then—I wake.

If only I could make the scores
I register between my snores,
And play them by the light of day,
I'd beat out Ouimet, Vardon, Ray.

If I could snooze and not wake up
I'd battle for the Lesley cup.
But such a game I only play
When I crawl in and hit the hay.

So I keep on, try out each club,
And still find I'm the same old dub.
I play the great and glorious game
Like some rheumatic, aged dame.

But if I only take a nap,
A smile of peace steals o'er my map.
I'm then a champ, again it seems.
My good scores come to me in dreams.

James P. Hughes suggests one other way to shoot low scores consistently–not in a reverie but in a fantasy still–in a poem that appeared in the December 1915 issue of *The American Golfer.*

♦ *Individual Golf*

He stood upon the link's first tee
    And made a straight and perfect drive.
His iron he sliced around a tree,
    Dead to the pin. Instead of five

He holed a single putt for three.

Another perfect shot was made—
    Two hundred fifty yards or more.
A midiron with a lofted blade
    He used to help his medal score,
For with it dead, the ball he laid.

Two threes he had to start the round.
    Next came a short and well trapped hole.
His drive, a cleek, rose from the ground
    Straight for the green and on the pole
He holed a two with smile profound.

Thus went his game in less than par—
    A record for all time, you guess.
No hook nor slice his score to mar;
    No balls in rough—all down in less
Than almost nothing—there you are.

No, gentle golfer, 'twas no dream
    In which this magic score was made,
Although at first it so would seem
    When former cards were cast in shade,
By this titanic play supreme.

But now the secret bare is shown
    Of how these threes and fours were done.
Some putts, of course, he could disown—
    In fact, he never claimed but one,
For this great golfer played alone.

Far greater than the best of clubs
    Is one lone pencil in the hand—
It saves a hundred strokes to dubs
    And proves a blessing in the land
Because it never counts the flubs.

Moral

When golfers tell of shots unknown,
Just ask them if they played alone.

Sir J. A. Hammerton in his book and poem, *The Rubaiyat of a Golfer*, included in part on the 7th Hole, describes a dream in stanza 15 to which most of us would ascribe.

Yet ~ can you name a Game with this to match?
In bed that night at home, *not* Colney Hatch,
    I lie a-dreaming how I best may bring
My Handicap of Eighteen down to Scratch!

"Colney Hatch," mentioned at the end of the second line, refers to The Middlesex County Pauper Lunatic Asylum at Colney Hatch, opened in 1851!

We conclude this 13th Hole with a "dream" poem by Billy Collins, the poet laureate of the United States from 2001–2003, and also an avid golfer.

♦ Night Golf

I remember the night I discovered,
Lying in bed in the dark,
That a few imagined holes of golf
Worked much better than a thousand sheep,

That the local links,
Not the cloudy pasture with its easy fence,
Was the greener path to sleep.

How soothing to stroll the inky fairways,
To skirt the moon-blanched bunkers
And hear the night owl in the woods.

Who cared about the score
When the club swung with the ease of air
And I glided from shot to shot
Over the mown and rolling ground,
Alone and drowsy with my weightless bag?

Eighteen small cups punched into the bristling grass,
Eighteen flags limp on their sticks
In the silent, windless dark,

But in the bedroom with its luminous clock
And propped-open windows,
I got only as far as the seventh
Before I nodded easily away—

The difficult seventh, "The Tester" they called it,
Where, just as on the earlier holes,
I tapped in, dreamily, for bird.

14th Hole. Weather and Seasons

The poem "Ballade of the Royal Game of Golf," written by Scottish golfer-poet-writer, Andrew Lang, was included on the 8th Hole. A stanza from that poem provides an ageless personal statement on golf as a game for all seasons as well as a game for a lifetime. That stanza is worth repeating to introduce the "climate" of this 14th Hole:

> "I hae play'd in the frost and the thaw,
>   I hae play'd since the year thirty-three,
> I hae play'd in the rain and the snaw,
>   And I trust I may play till I dee."

The Scottish golfer has always been a hardy soul playing through bad weather and worse. Rudyard Kipling, the famous English author and poet, whose poem "Mine Sweepers" was included on the 10th Hole, was, likewise, a hardy golf enthusiast. He is credited with inventing the game of "snow golf" while playing with red balls in Vermont during the winter months. He lived in Brattleboro for four years, from 1892 to 1896.

However, Kipling noted that snow golf was "not altogether a success because there were no limits to a drive; the ball might skid two miles down the long slope to the Connecticut river."

While in Vermont, Kipling once hosted Sir Arthur Conan Doyle, whose poem about the joys of golf was included on the 3rd Hole. Doyle stayed with Kipling for two days, apparently bringing along his golf clubs, because during his stay, Doyle gave Kipling "an extended golf lesson."

Though Kipling wrote many poems, I could find only three that related to golf – "Mine Sweepers," "The Sages of the Links" and "Verses on Games." This last poem consists of twelve stanzas with each focused on a specific game, one for every month. But even when limited to four lines, Kipling shows that he understood the subtleties of hitting a golf ball.

♦ October (Golf)

Why Golf is art and art is Golf
 We have not far to seek—
So much depends upon the lie,
 So much upon the cleek.

Kipling may have chosen to couple golf with October since, in New England, October signals that the end of golf season is near. Francis Bowler Keene, who graduated from Harvard University in 1880, a contemporary of Kipling, wrote a poem that should appeal especially to golfers who live in snowy areas of the country. In his title, Keene uses the word "monody," meaning lament, to set his tone.

♦ A Golfer's Monody, After the First Snowfall

No greens, no tees;
    No fragrant breeze;
No harmony of happy-hearted birds;
    No verdure deep;
    No roaming sheep;
No faithful collies, watchful of their herds;
    No sunny glade;
    No woodland shade;
No ferny path beneath the rustling trees;
    No springy turf;
    No murmuring surf;
No passing hum of honey-laden bees;
    No motors fleet;
    No golfers' meet;
No lazy caddies lolling day by day;
    No warning call;
    No flying ball;
No contest in the fine and friendly fray;
    No clubs to wield;
    No drive afield;
No plaudits as the ball, far-driven flies;
    No close-trimmed lawn;
    No bunker's yawn;
No hidden hazards lurking with bad lies;
    No brassy swift;
    No niblick's lift;
No ringing click of iron, clear and clean;
    No cleek's true swing;
    No mashie's fling;
No careful putt along the velvet green;
    No Club-nights gay;

No moonlit bay;
No dinners marked by mirth and merry jest;
    No music bright;
    No dancers light;
No broad verandah thronged with happy guests;
    No winding walks;
    No golfers' talks;
No genuine delight for every member;
    No matches more;
    No games galore;
    No joyous strife;
    No zest in life;
       November.

Robert K Risk, the Scottish poet, whom we have previously met on the 7th and 12th Holes, offers us this paean, a song of exultation, from the non-playing wife's view of life between golf seasons.

♦ A Paean for the Winter

Gone is the time when by the sad, grey sea
    I waited patiently two weary rounds,
Gone are the days he spent 'twixt green and tee,
    And Golf is now restrained within due bounds
For Summer fled I do not sigh "Alack-
A-day:" I'm very glad it can't come back.

Gone are the evenings when he used to start,
    After a scrambling meal—I hate high-teaing—
"Forgetful of the office and the mart,"
    And also of his spouse's very being;
His love for an insensate ball and cleek
Made me a widow six days in each week.

And now at last from Sunday until Friday,
    He recognizes that he has a wife
Whose sole concern is not to keep things tidy
    And share the merest fraction of his life,
Providing just the things he likes for dinner,
In case his bunker-work should make him thinner.

And now, when Winter fires and lamps are lit,
    I have some respite from his golfing jargon,
Which, frankly, I don't understand a bit—
    It bored me nightly in the months that are gone;
Sometimes for a whole day, in winter weather,
He will forget his mania altogether.

Therefore that "scintillating constellation,"
    The next Spring Meeting, never mocks my eye;
I can forget my old exasperation—
    Now his Midsummer madness has gone by.
But if next year he flouts me for a "foursome,"
I shall burn all his clubs, or else divorce him.

Risk may have gotten inspiration for this poem from a novel called *The Sorrows of a Golfer's Wife* written by Mrs. Edward Kennard and published in 1896. According to the late Joseph S. F. Murdock, the fabled golf book collector, Mrs. Kennard's novel was the first golf book written by a woman. She published a sequel, *The Golf Lunatic and His Cycling Wife*, in 1902. I could not determine if this novel had biographical roots beyond the fact that Mrs. Kennard was, in fact, a sometimes cyclist.

Back to the weather and a rather ironic take on a beautiful day for golf, Bert Leston Taylor, the *Chicago Tribune* columnist, asks this poetic question:

◆ Why

Why, when the sun is gold
   The weather fine,
The air (this phrase is old)
   Like Gascon wine;—

Why, when the leaves are red,
   And yellow too,
And when (as has been said)
   The skies are blue;—

Why, when all things promote
   One's peace and joy
A joy that is (to quote)
   Without alloy;—

Why, when a man's well off,
   Happy and gay,
Why must he go play golf
   And spoil his day?

Most golfers in lands of four distinct seasons try to play at least until November. Then many stow away their clubs for the winter, with a few promising themselves that come spring and clement weather, they will no longer "spoil" their days. However, as all incurable golfers know and as Henry Walcott Boynton affirmed on the 7th Hole:

Indeed, indeed, Repentance oft before
I swore—but it was Winter when I swore,
   And then and then came Spring, and Club-in-hand
I hasten'd forth for one Round—one Round more.

15th Hole. Golf Songs

In earlier times, golf songs were part of the fabric of golf. The word "goff" was mentioned in a song as early as 1671, as noted on The Practice Tee. The 1st Hole ends with some lines from the song "Far and Sure"; in addition, the 5th Hole begins with the first four lines of a song called "The Links o' Inner-leven." The sub-title of this song reads, "Sung at the Autumn Meeting of the Innerleven Golfing Club, 1841." The song's last eight lines, with a little updating, would still seem to work for today's members of the Leven Golfing Society, an amal-gamation of Innerleven and the Leven Golf Club.

> And when the e'ening grey sat doun
> I'd cast aside my tacket shoon*,   spiked shoes
> And crack* o' putter, cleek, and spoon   talk
>   Wi' a friend at Innerleven.

Syne* o'ver a glass o' Cameron Brig   Then
A nightcap we could doucely* swig,   sedately
Laughing at Conservative and Whig,
    By the Links o' Innerleven.

Another Innerleven Golf Club song, this one sung at the autumn meeting in 1848, hails the introduction of the gutta percha ball. The "Guttie" had been first introduced at St. Andrews earlier that year and was modified over the next few years to improve its performance.

In the beginning, Gutties were hammered with a sharp-edged hammer into a consistent pattern throughout. Later, handmade balls gave way to balls formed with metal presses. This change in manufacture made golf balls more affordable for the lower-income golfer. The introduction of the Guttie signaled the demise of the "feathery," the leather-covered ball stuffed with feathers or hair, and was one of the first major turning points in golf technology.

The five stanza song "In Praise of *Gutta Percha*" begins:

Of a' the changes that of late
Have shaken Europe's social state—
Let wondering politicians prate,*   babble
   And 'bout them mak a wark a'—* make a work all
A subject mair* congenial here,   more
And dearer to a Golfer's ear
I sing—the changes brought round last year
   By balls of *Gutta Percha!*

Europe in the late 1840's witnessed both the rise in the influence of Karl Marx and the start of the second French Republic. But whatever the song's reference, its lyricist clearly has his priorities straight. The third stanza would have made good advertising copy had there been golf magazines at that time.

Hail, *Gutta Percha*, precious gum!
O'er Scotland's links lang may ye bum;*   long may you bounce
Some purse-proud billies* haw and hum,   fellows
    And say ye're douf at fleein';*   poor at flying
But let them try ye fairly out,
Wi' only balls for days about,
Your merits they will loudly tout
    And own they hae been leein'.*   lying

I could not find a comparable song about the Haskell, a one-piece rubber ball, introduced about fifty years later. Haskells looked like Gutties but gave the average golfer an extra twenty yards from the tee. Sounds familiar.

Recall that "Far and Sure," the name of the 1ˢᵗ Hole, was also the title of a song by Sheriff Logan and another by Edward Atherton. The motto was turned around in "A Golfing Song" by a Scottish 19ᵗʰ century poet, James Ballantine. This song was written in the same time period as Logan's and may have been the first to suggest the still popular idea of leaving work early to play a little golf.

♦ *A Golfing Song*

"Come, leave your dingy desks and shops,
    Ye sons of ancient Reekie,*   Edinburgh
And by green fields and sunny slopes,
    For a healthy pastime seek ye,
Don't bounce about your '*dogs of war,*'
    Nor at our *shinties** scoff, boys,   precursor to hockey
But learn our motto, '*Sure and Far,*'
    Then come and play at Golf, Boys."

The song's chorus links it with a particular golf course, the Bruntsfield Links in Edinburgh:

Three rounds at Bruntsfield Links will chase
All murky vapours off, boys;
And nothing can your sinews brace
Like the glorious game of Golf, boys.

At the time this song was sung, the Bruntsfield Links consisted of six holes so three rounds would have totaled a
standard eighteen.

The later half of the 19th century also marked the rise of
the musical comedy in London. An early favorite was Gilbert
and Sullivan's *HMS Pinafore*. One of the songs in that musical
was titled "The First Lord's Song," where the first stanza may
be familiar:

When I was a lad I served a term
As office boy to an attorney's firm
I cleaned the windows and I swept the floor
And I polished up the handle of the big front door
  I polished up that handle so carefully
  That now I am the Ruler of the Queen's Navy.

In a small thin book, *Lays of the Links*, edited by T. Ross
Stewart and published in 1895, an unknown poet provides a
clever parody.

♦ *The Winner of the Queen's Trophee*

When I was a lad I served a term
As 'prentice boy to a club-maker's firm;
Tied the whippings and I boiled the glue,
And I polished up the irons till they looked like new.
  I polished up the irons so successfulee
  That now I am the Winner of the Queen's Trophee!

As apprentice boy I made such a mark,

That I once was taken for a man called Park;
I could fix in a rivet and put on a new head,
I could varnish all the brassies and fill in fresh lead.
    I varnished all the brassies so splendidlee
    That now I am the Winner of the Queen's Trophee!

As a first-class artificer I made such a name
That my clubs were purchased by exponents of the game;
I could get half-a-guinea for a special shaft,
And my heads were a model of my handicraft.
    I charged such a price for my artilleree
    That now I am the Winner of the Queen's Trophee!

Of golfing knowledge I acquired such a grip,
That they offered to take me into partnership;
This offer I considered, but at last declined,
And I set myself to practise with an ardent mind.
    I practised up the game so ardentlee
    That now I am the Winner of the Queen's Trophee!

I became such a swell that I was sent
To represent my country in a tournament;
I beat all the records of the local men
And they never thought of asking me to play again.
    I beat all their records so disgracefullee
    That now I am the Winner of the Queen's Trophee!

Now amateurs all, whoever you may be,
If you're anxious to rise to the top of the tree,
In every kind of hazard keep your head quite cool
And be careful to be guided by this golden rule:—
    Take half the holes in four, and the other half in three:
    And you all may be the Winner of the Queen's Trophee!

The December 1895 issue of *The Golfer*, America's first golf magazine, published in Boston, included the words and music of "Song of the Golfers," said to be "the first American golf song ever published." It was written by Frank J. Bonnelle who also wrote poetry for the magazine. The music was composed by Benjamin E. Woolf, better known for writing the opera *Westward Ho!* The first verse began,

> We love the royal ancient game
> In golf we take delight
> We wield our clubs for fun and fame,
> With all our skill and might.

And the third and last verse ends,

> Kind Nature's aid we aye invoke,
> We breathe her zephyrs pure
> We put our soul in every stroke—
> Our motto "Far and Sure."

Both the composer and lyricist were well known at the time, but it is doubtful that the song caught on, in spite of its centuries old motto.

In 1903, *The Golf Song Book* was published in Edinburgh. It was edited by Rev. John Kerr with Music by J. Kenyon Lees. The book consisted of "Classic golf songs set to music." Among them were Arthur Conan Doyle's "A Lay of the Links," from the 3rd Hole and three by John Thomson, who wrote the story of "the Skipper" told on the 11th Hole. In the Foreword to the book, Rev. Kerr wrote,

> ". . . the songs of golf are legion. The drawback is that these songs are not generally set to music . . . It is to help on this good cause, to enable golfers to enjoy the praise of Golf and to fight their battles o'er again, to forget their defeats and rejoice in their victories, that this Collection has been made, in the

hope that it may at least form the nucleus of a collection, the absence of which seemed to be a reproach to the golfing community."

Also in the early 20th century, Grantland Rice wrote a poem, "Songs of Dufferdom," that masqueraded as a song. It is doubtful that Rice had music in mind when he wrote these verses, but, by stretching some words a little, the verses can be sung to the melody of "Home on the Range," without the chorus. Thus, had it been a real song, Rice's poem might have been called "Home in the Pit!"

♦ Songs of Dufferdom

The friendly pit, so full of sand,
    I love through May and June;
Take a niblick in my hand
    And spend the afternoon.

The fairway's green and long and wide
    Where one can play with par;
And yet somehow I'd rather hide
    Down where the heel prints are.

Though others scorn its sandy showers
    Or turn from it and flee,
I've spent so many, many hours
    That it's like home to me.

Let's add a chorus to make the would-be song complete.

Home, home in the pit
Where it's most painful to play
Where seldom is heard
An encouraging word

And my score climbs higher all day.

This hole would not be complete without including a golf song that was actually sung and recorded by a popular singer. "Straight Down the Middle" was put on record by Bing Crosby, the great crooner and a pretty fair golfer. Crosby hosted the first National Pro-Amateur Golf Championship (now the AT&T) at Rancho Santa Fe Golf Club in California, the event's location prior to World War II. Sam Snead won the first tournament and received a check for $500.

Crosby was inducted into the World Golf Hall of Fame in 1978. He had died a year earlier just after completing a round of golf in Madrid, Spain.

♦ Straight Down the Middle

F O R E!

Straight down the middle
It went straight down the middle
Then it started to hook just a wee wee bit
That's when my caddie lost sight of it
That little white pellet has never been found to this day
But it went straight down the middle like they say

Whack down the fairway
It went smack down the fairway
Then it started to slice just a smidge off line
It headed for two but it bounced off nine
My caddie says long as you're still in the state you're okay
Yes it went straight down the middle quite a ways

The sun was never brighter
The greens were never greener
And I was never keener to play

I heard it came down the middle
It went zing down the middle
Oh the life of a golfer is not all gloom
There's always the lies in the locker room
And I'm in my glory when wrapped in a towel I say
That it went straight down the middle today

Oh the life of a golfer is not all gloom
Though they charge just for listening in the locker room
But I'm in my glory when wrapped in a towel I say
That it went straight down the middle
Where it wound up is a riddle
But it went straight down the middle far away.

16th Hole. The Women's Game

The women's game began with Mary Stuart, Queen of Scots, regarded by golf historians as the first woman player in Scotland. However, her passion for the game created "scandal and suspicion" in February 1567 when she was seen playing golf beside Seton Castle in East Lothian, shortly after the murder of her husband, Lord Darnley. She and Darnley were the parents of the golfing James VI of Scotland who became James I of England upon the death of Elizabeth I. King James I was the first English monarch to play the game, having brought his clubs south of the border in 1603.

A short time after Darnley's murder, Mary was forced to abdicate the Scottish throne. For her remaining 19 years she was held under house arrest by her cousin, Queen Elizabeth I of England, most likely ending her playing days. Ultimately, she was tried and convicted for treasonous activities against her cousin's throne and was beheaded on February 8, 1587.

All in all, a rather dismal and foreboding start for the women's game.

Early women golfers are not mentioned in print until the 1790's. In a section of an obscure report, the *Statistical Accounts of Scotland: Inveresk, County of Edinburgh* titled "Occupations of Women," the following is said about "fish wives":

"As the women do the work of men, their manners are masculine, and their strength and activity is equal to their work. Their amusements are of the masculine kind. On holidays they frequently play at golf . . ."

According to the early 20th century golf historian Robert Browning, these women played their golf at Musselburgh. In fact, the Club minutes of December 14, 1810, about twenty years after the entry in the *Statistical Accounts*, include the following:

"The Club resolve to present by subscription a new Creel and Shawl [a small fish basket] to the best female golfer who plays on the annual occasion on 1st Jan. next, old style (12th Jan. new), to be intimated to the Fish Ladies by the Officer of the Club."

However, for the most part in the early 19th century, golf on the east coast of Scotland was strictly a man's game. Consider these four lines from the poem "The Golfiad" by George Fullerton Carnegie, from his book *Golfiana*.

The game is ancient—manly—and employs
In its departments, women, men, and boys;
Men play the game, the boys the clubs convey,
And lovely woman gives the prize away.

The first real step in the development of women's golf came when "the ladies" began to form their own golf clubs. The first was the St. Andrews Ladies' Golf Club, organized in 1867. However, on competition days for the first thirty years, the Club conducted its affairs from tents. Finally, in 1898 permission was obtained to erect a shelter.

In the late 19th century as more women seriously took up the game, the Ladies' Golf Union was formed. The purpose of the union was to act as the governing body for ladies' amateur golf in Great Britain and Ireland. In 1893, its inaugural year, the Union conducted the first British Ladies' Championship at Lytham St. Anne's, located on the northwestern coast of England just south of Blackpool. The winner was Lady Margaret Scott. The Championship was deemed a great success even though just prior to the matches, Horace Hutchinson, one of the greatest amateur golfers and golf minds of the time, wrote:

"Women never have and never can unite to push any scheme to success. They are bound to fall out and quarrel on the smallest or no provocation; they are built that way! They will never go through one Ladies Championship with credit. Tears will bedew, if wigs do not bestrew, the green. Constitutionally and physically women are unfitted for golf."

Hutchinson clearly had a problem with women playing golf. But events would prove him wrong regarding the Championship and wrong again regarding women golfers in general.

The second year, the Ladies' Championship was played at Littlestone-on-Sea, on the South East coast of England. This Championship was won again by Lady Margaret, the best of the early women amateurs in Great Britain and the winner of the first four championships.

Inexplicably, Lady Margaret and a number of her competitors were memorialized in a poem said to be "found one morning during the 1894 Championship lying on the floor of the club-house." According to Mabel Stringer, one of the players mentioned in the poem, in her book *Golfing Reminiscences*, "The original is, or was, preserved among the archives of the Littlestone Ladies' Club."

The untitled poem is thought to have been written by some of the women competitors. All the golfers mentioned by name or description can be identified. I have done so for a few of the more famous women. Because this was the first golf poem focused entirely on women golfers, I have included it in its entirety.

Sixty-four ladies, golfers all,
Stout and large and thin and small,
For the championship fought at Littlestone,
To let the champion there be shown.

Dear "Auntie Drake" of sturdy make,
With heart so large and tender;
Tho' named a drake, my word you'll take,
She's of the female gender.

And "Niecey" too looms into view,
Armed with her brassy trusty;
And if she's down, she ne'er will frown
Nor turn the least bit crusty.

Now Starkie-Bence, with drives immense,
Clears both canal and bunker,
But on the Green, it will be seen,
The little hole will funk her.

Dame Cameron will hammer on,
In spite of all disaster.

With stately mien, a golfer keen,
There's few who can outlast her.

E. Catterall might scatter all,
If in the fateful draw
She had not got the champion "Scott,"
Who is a gowfer braw.

Now Lottie Dod, so neatly shod,
Stands forth upon the tee;
On tennis green she is the queen,
At golf what will she be?

But Peregrine Birch can't be left in the lurch,
She's got a rod in pickle;
D. Jeffrey, she, 'twixt you and me,
Doth much my fancy tickle.

Mrs. Stanley Stubbs, on the green has rubs
Which she takes with a smile benign;
Though golfing of late has turned her pate,
Yet singing is more in her line.

A dame from France now meets our glance,   (Mrs. Tennant)
Round whom opinion rages,
And whether she will beat I.P.   (Issette Pearson)
Will be seen in final stages.

Mrs. Stewart, a golfer who grew at
A forest near Tunbridge Wells;
So neat in her play, 'tis needless to say
She'll make a good match for the swells.

Our thoughts now linger around Miss Stringer,
The local Captain genial
We'll long recall her care for all,
She's slaved like any menial.

The famous "Lena", have you seen her   (Miss Lena Thomson)
Deadly short approaches?
When these you see, you will agree
This golfer Tom Dunn coaches.

As Mrs. Willock, drives a hillock
Somebody call out "Ah!
Now what is that?" "You silly flat,
She is a rising star."

Mrs. Hoare from the West must play her best
In meeting a Wimbledon crack,
She must drive a long ball, or she will feel small
With this golfer whom caddies do back.

Miss Terry is a strong one, very,
She'll "terrify" the field;
A golfer she from Anne's-by-Sea,
Who can her driver wield.

A Southdown player, who is not a stayer, (Miss Blanche Martin)
As "Mashie" arrives on the scene;
In writing she'll shine, more than in the golf line,
For "divots" she's noted, I ween.

The Wimbledon pet is Miss Issette,   (Issette Pearson)
Who plays a real good game;
Lady Margaret Scott might prove too hot
Unless a "dark horse" came.

In 1899, the first golf poetry book published in America was, oddly enough, *The Golf Girl*, with verses by Samuel Minturn Peck. It was hardly a book, being only fifteen pages long. However, in addition to a few poems by Peck, it includes four "exquisite chromolithographs of The Golf Girl in four different enchanting golfing outfits." These illustrations were by the famous children's illustrator Maud Humphrey, the mother of the actor Humphrey Bogart.

Peck, Alabama's first poet laureate, described "The Golf Girl" in the first poem titled "Rondeau." The title actually refers to the particular rhyming structure that the poem takes–fifteen lines with only two rhymes–similar to some French lyrical poems of the fourteenth and fifteenth centuries. The poem itself seems to carry on the tradition and attitude of George Fullerton Carnegie. Again, I include it only for historical purposes as the first poem by an American poet to mention a woman golfer.

♦ Rondeau

The Golf Girl, Sirs, I sing to you;
Her sun-ripe cheeks, her eyes like dew.
No Amaryllis in the shade
Of beechen boughs—no nymph e'er strayed
In Arcady as fair—or true.

The world desired a woman new—
The curtain's up. Advance and view,
In hale and simple charm arrayed,
    The Golf Girl.

The brightest, best of Beauty's crew,
In winsomeness she works no rue
As she on Seton's links who played—
How Mary Stuart's charm would fade
Before the sweetest ever blew,
    The Golf Girl.

Peck's book ends with the poem "The Lassie That Swiped With A Cleek," the story of a suitor and his lost love, "the lassie," who could actually play. We pick up the story in the third stanza when the suitor's rival appears. The lassie's suitor speaks.

> I recall we were playing at singles,
>   And none but the caddies were nigh.
> But—alas! How the bitter commingles—
>   Soon a stranger—to me—loitered by!
> He lingered—and wrathfully tingles
>   My blood as I think of his "cheek,"
>   Admiring her stance,
>   Or exchanging a glance
> With the lassie that swiped with a cleek.
>
> It nettled me so—this intrusion—
>   My clubs—wooden, iron, and brass—
> I mixed in a hapless confusion
>   No madman could hope to surpass.
> If my ankles escaped a contusion,
>   I owed it to luck, in my pique,
>   As he laughed in his glee
>   When she holed out in three,
> The lassie that swiped with a cleek.

Skipping on to the last stanza, we find, predictably, that the intruder wins out.

> But enough. When the sun had descended,
>   And the links by long shadows was crost,
> I found with the game that had ended
>   That more than one match I had lost.
> Not with me but another she wended;
>   And the varlet whose sorrow I seek
>   He captured—the wag—
>   Both the heart and the bag
> Of the lassie that swiped with a cleek!

The use of ridicule and sarcasm were two of the few weapons that women could wield to get back at these cloying male poets. Amelia Adams Harrington, clearly an early feminist, wrote these lines:

◆ *It's a Great Life*

Hello, dear, how are you?
Glad you came around.
Fred's out at the Country Club
Batting up the ground.

Did you go to Martha's
Fred came in too late.
Played 'til it was pitchy dark,
Forgot we had a date.

Oh, you leave tomorrow?
I would like it there.
Freddie won't hear of it, for
The course is only fair.

We are coming 'round to see
You and Mr. Haines.
Possibly on Sunday
That is—if it rains.

Some male poets also took the women's side. One was J.P. McEvoy, the creator of the comic strip Dixie Dugan and originator of the quote often attributed to Mark Twain: "Whenever the impulse to exercise comes over me, I lie down until it passes away." His poem was published in *Lyrics of the Links* in 1921.

♦ The Stranger

Who's that stranger, mother dear?
Look, he knows us . . . Ain't he queer?"

"Hush, my own, don't talk so wild;
He's your father, dearest child!"

"He's my father? No such thing!
Father died away last Spring!"

"Father didn't die, you dub!
Father joined a golfing club.

"But they've closed the club, so he
Has no place to go you see—

"No place left for him to roam—
That is why he's coming home.

"Kiss him . . . he won't bite you child;
All them golfing guys look wild."

Robert Risk's poem "A Paean for Winter," included on the 14th Hole, would also fit nicely here with the non-playing wife's view of life as a golf widow "six days in each week."

I end with one more Clerihew capsulizing how far women's golf in America has advanced since "The Golf Girl."

♦ Michele Wie

Michele Wie
May still want to see
If there's a chance
To beat pros who wear pants.

17th Hole. An Epic Poem

SPRING'S FIRST BALL

A prolific writer and poet, Clinton Scollard was a professor of English literature at Hamilton College in Clinton, New York, for eight years. In 1923 he published a ninety-eight page book, *The Epic of Golf*, which contains a poem of ninety stanzas, illustrated with eight drawings. Epic poems, such as Scollard's, are long heroic narratives that date back to ancient times. Three of the most famous epics, of course, are the *Iliad* and the *Odyssey* by Homer and the *Aeneid* by Virgil.

Lord Byron, the famous early 19th century English Romantic poet, in a satiric stanza from his poem "Don Juan," tells us just what makes a poem "epic."

My poem's epic, and is meant to be
    Divided in twelve books; each book containing,
With Love, and War, a heavy gale at sea,
    A list of ships, and captains, and kings reigning,
New characters; the episodes are three;
    A panoramic view of Hell's in training,
After the style of Virgil and of Homer,
    So that my name of Epic's no misnomer.

Scollard's *Epic* chronicles the travails of a novice golfer. True to form, the story unfolds in three episodes, titled "Initiation," "Participation" and "Realization." It ends with an "Envoy," a short final section. The "hero" narrates the poem. As with the other long works included in this book, I have summarized the story and provide some illustrative stanzas. [Interestingly, Scollard's poem has the same rhyme scheme as the *Rubaiyat* on the 7th Hole.]

Scollard's narrator begins:

Upon the morning of a tonic day
When kingcups danced along the banks of May,
    By what is now an unremembered lure
I was won forth the game of Golf to play.

It is a joy to see the eager Spring
Stride o'er the land with flowery triumphing;
    "Who loves it not," I thought, "at soul is poor,
As for the game—that's quite another thing!"

Unto a spot they called the "tee," we went,
With many a strange and uncouth implement;
    My sponsor builded up a little sand
And placed the ball, and then looked well content.

There was a place afar they dubbed "the green"
Beyond a grassy, rillet-cut ravine;

"That's the first hole!" with gracious wave of hand,
My friend assured me as I scanned the scene.

Upon the ball he fixed a steadfast eye,
And, with a desperate air of do or die,
    Wagged twice or thrice with his long club of wood,
And next with all his might and main let fly.

The narrator's "sponsor," described in the poem as a
friend, then proceeds to hit a wayward tee shot that "swooped
ravine-ward sudden, swift and sheer."

Then straightway burst the Maytime air upon
Words, loud and lurid words, one after one;
    I was discovering early, I avow,
How vivid is the golfer's lexicon.

It was now the "hero's" turn at the tee, and with beginner's luck, after several whiffs, he connects. His friend's
predictable response,

"A fluke!" he cried, his jealousy revealed;
"Truly," I murmured, and his pride was healed.
    A fluke it was beyond a shade of doubt,
But from that day and hour my fate was sealed.

So the novice is quickly hooked, but as you would expect,
as he continues, his play is up and down.

I pulled, I sliced, I foozled, and, in fine,
The path was blazed—the divots were the sign—
    Where I had passed, but when I fairly hit
The battered sphere, what ecstasy was mine!

Well," cried my friend, when finally we came
To the last hole, "What think you of the game?"

With eye dispassionate I scanned the course,
And boldly turned and said, "Put up my name!"

And that night in bed, as in the dream poetry on the 13th Hole:

In visions then did I with Vardon vie;
And, as I lay, there seemed to be no "lie"
    Beyond the wondrous prowess of my reach
With any iron that I chose to try.

In the second Canto [section], titled "Participation," the narrator is initially faced with the problem of purchasing clubs. His advisors, like the Golf Channel's paid programs, have all the answers:

And now behold me, since the die was cast,
More sore perplexed than ever in the past;
    My complement of clubs I needs must choose,
And round me mentors gathered thick and fast.

"This," one declared, "you cannot do without;"
"That," said another "helps you when in doubt;"
    "This club," another cried, "you'll often use;
And that will aid in many a bitter bout!"

Though our hero's time is long ago, his response still has a familiar ring.

As does a wanderer in a wildering maze,
Deeper and deeper grew my desperate daze,
    Till when I closed my eyes in sheer despair
A host of clubs went whirling dizzy ways.

Then came a golfer on whom knowledge sate,
Who put a surcease upon all debate;

"Each mon," remarked he, with deliberate air,
"Duffer or no, should follow his ain gait*."   own way

And so the narrator buys his first set of clubs.

Thus was I left unto my own device,
Save for the dealer, and I paid his price;
   But what cared I? With joy my visage gleamed
As does a boy's who tries forbidden ice.

Armed with new clubs, the narrator practices and begins
to play, poorly at first.

Then, after long and wearisome delay,
I fell upon a brilliant burst of play;
   I did not know, alas, I did not know.
Like every dog, the duffer has his day!

Still he senses that there is more to learn, "men have
surely writ/of golfing both with wisdom and with wit..."
The poem continues:

Astonished was I at the tomes I found
In fitting hues, and hues unfitting, bound;
   But woe is me! The longer that I read,
The deeper I in mental muddle drowned!

Scollard's characterization is all the more interesting since
this work was published in 1923 when the number of golf
instruction books was minuscule compared to today. Regardless, few or many, the books did not help. The narrator then
recognizes, as many of us have, the primacy of experience:

Much may they know, these penmen who declaim
On this and that, and all with goodly aim;

But Dame Experience is the teacher, she,
When all is written, best expounds the game.

By the end of the second section, the narrator is fully immersed in the game. In the final two stanzas he eloquently describes his state of dufferdom:

For, though I falter on the path to fame,
And ne'er in medal-play behold my name,
   Nor cut a figure on the winning side,
A solace to my soul remains the game!

The game remains; and I shall swear thereby,
What e'er the season, and what e'er the "lie,"
   Although it sorely crucify my pride,
And I remain a duffer till I die!

In the third section, time has moved on to autumn, and the narrator describes a match played and lost. At the start:

Halved is the hole, and now the Woodside dares
Our dual trial of its pits and snares;
   What sloughs of sorrow and what perils here
Lie hid to catch the wariest unawares!

And at the end:

And so the hours slip swiftly one by one,
While westward flames the red October sun;
   The hills cast long cool shadows o'er the dale;
Holed is the last ball and the game is done.

A short concluding Canto of ten stanzas ends the epic. Scollard begins this section by describing beautifully the mystical divide that separates golfers and non-golfers:

You, the Ungolfing, who have never seen
The lofted ball fall dead upon the green.
    Who have not known the skilly putter's bliss,
Alas, alas, what sterile fields you glean!

Among Scollard's concluding stanzas are three that recall "the
seasons" poetry of the 14th Hole.

Yes, he can wait until the vernal chord
Softly smitten, and the umbered sward
    Quickens beneath the sun's renewing fire.
And stripling Spring is Winter's overlord.

Then feel his feet the tempting turf once more,
While down the distance floats his ringing "fore!"
    And he is brother to the hale desire
That is of all reviving things the core.

Others may catch the scattered scrap and shard
Of exultation, but to them is barred
    The keen elation that the Golfer knows
When Spring's first ball is teed and driven hard.

These last two lines illustrate once again how a poet's few
carefully chosen words can speak so personally to every avid
golfer:

"The keen elation that the Golfer knows
When Spring's first ball is teed and driven hard."

18th Hole. Golf Poetry's Beginnings – First Mention, First Poem, First Book

We have reached the eighteenth hole, an appropriate point from which to look back and consider the beginnings of golf poetry. The earliest poem known to include a reference to golf is "The Muses Threnodie, or Mirthfull Mournings on the Death of Master Gall" by Henry Adamson, published in Edinburgh in 1638. Adamson's poem is thought to be the first printed set of verses to refer to the game, discounting the dating of *Auld Wullie's Almanack,* quoted from at the beginning of the 4th Hole.

"The Muses Threnodie" consists of nine sections, titled "First Muse," "Second Muse" up to the "Ninth Muse." The

poem mourns the death of Master Gall, "a committed
sportsman who regularly played golf" and clearly a dear friend
of Adamson's. The following is the short section from the
First Muse in which the golf reference occurs:

And ye my clubs, you must no more prepare
To make your balls flee whistling in the air,
But hing* your heads, and bow your   hang
   crooked crags*,   necks
And dress you all in sackcloth and in rags,
No more to see the sun, nor fertile fields,
But closely keep your mourning in your bields*;   shelters
And for your part the trible* to you take,   treble
And when you cry, make all your crags to crake*,   shake
And shiver when you sing, alas! for Gall!
Ah, if our mourning might thee now recall!

    Thomas Kincaid, a medical student in Edinburgh, kept a
diary from January 1687 to December 1688 that has survived.
According to Olive M Geddes, Senior Curator in the National
Library of Scotland, Kincaid "meditated" on a number of
subjects including "theology, literature, politics, music and
sport." Kincaid's interest in sports is focused primarily on golf
and archery. He played golf during the winter months usually
at the Leith Links, though his diary mentions playing at the
Bruntsfield Links as well.
    Besides being a student of medicine, Kincaid also seems
to have been a student of golf. In various diary entries he
describes his golf swing. He also discusses his golfing equipment, methods to repair clubs, experiments with golf balls and
ideas about a system of handicapping. In an entry on February
9, 1687, Kincaid pens what is likely the first poem entirely
devoted to golf. He writes, "I digested the rules of playing at
the golve into verse thus:"

Gripe fast stand with your left leg first not farr
Incline your back and shoulders but beware
You raise them not when back the club you bring
Make all the motion with your bodies swinge
And shoulders, holding still the muscles bent   (5)
Play slowly first till you the way have learnt
At such lenth hold the club as fitts your strength
The lighter head requires the longer lenth
That circle wherein moves your club and hands
At forty five degrees from Th[e] horizon stands   (10)
What at on[e] stroak to effectuat you dispaire
Seek only 'gainst the nixt it to prepare.

With these twelve lines Kincaid establishes himself as golf's first swing instructor. Lines nine and ten make him the first golfer to write about the swing plane that so consumed Ben Hogan. Moreover, he warns early about keeping your head still and in the last two lines makes what must be the first reference to the mental game.

We know that the eighteenth hole is where amateur and professional alike feel the most pressure—the amateur to make a score, the professional to win the tournament. Recall from "The Lay for the Troubled Golfer" on the 4th Hole:

I'd an easy five for a seventy-nine—in sight of the golden goal—
An easy five and I took an eight—an eight on the eighteenth hole!

But eighteenth-hole dramas actually go back to the beginning of golf poetry.

In 1743, a writer and legal clerk, Thomas Mathison, published a mock-heroic poem, an epic in which the drama peaks on the eighteenth hole. The mythical match is played on the Leith Link between Castalio and Pygmalion, the "heroic" combatants of the tale. Mathison's poem, *The Goff – a Heroi-*

Comical Poem in Three Cantos, is a 358-line poem first printed by
J. Cochran and Company in Edinburgh.

The Goff is commonly referred to as the first separately
printed golf book. After its initial publication, it was published
again twenty years later in 1763 by James Reid, a bookseller.
And a third edition was published in 1793 in Edinburgh by
Peter Hill. This version contained "A Few Notes and Illustrations." One of the few surviving third edition copies was sold
in 1998 for $80,500.

In 1981 the United States Golf Association published a
single facsimile edition of all three versions, the first two
reproduced in full size, the third at eighty percent of full size.

You need not go beyond the first line of *The Goff* to iden-
tify the comic intent of Mathison. Virgil's famous epic poem,
the *Aeneid,* begins, "Arms, and the man I sing, who, forc'd by
fate . . .," while *The Goff* begins:

> GOFF, and the *Man,* I sing, who, em'lous, plies
> The jointed club; whose balls invade the skies;
> Who from *Edina's* tow'rs, his peaceful home,
> In quest of fame o'er *Letha's* plains did roam.

According to the National Library of Scotland's interpre-
tation, "*Edina's* tow'rs" and "*Letha's* plains" conjure up mock-
heroic images of the towers at Troy and the famous river of
forgetfulness in the Greek underworld. "Edina" refers to
Edinburgh and "Letha" to Leith and the Leith Links. The
protagonists in this "golfing clash of the titans" are Pygmalion, who is said to be Mathison, and Castalio, identified as an
Edinburgh book seller, Alexander Dunning. Again, according
to the National Library, Mathison, "was a lawyer who moved
in the upper echelons of Edinburgh society" and was also a
capable golfer.

The opponents are dramatically introduced about a third of the way through the first Canto:

> Forth rush'd *Castalio* and his daring foe,
> Both arm'd with clubs, and eager for the blow.
> Of finest ash *Castalio's* shaft was made,
> Pond'rous with lead, and fenc'd with horn the head,
> (The work of *Dickson*, who in *Letha* dwells,
> And in the art of making clubs excels),

"Dickson" is Andrew Dickson, a famous club-maker of that time. As a boy he may have carried the Duke of York's golf clubs. Thus, it is possible that he was present at the first international golf match described on the 1st Hole. One of Dickson's long-nosed putters was sold at a New York Sotheby's auction in September 2007 for $181,000.

The match between Pygmalion and Castalio is played on Leith Links. A close reading of the poem indicates that it began about noon and lasted until late afternoon. The Links had only five holes at the time and at the end of three rounds, towards the end of the second Canto in the poem, Castalio [Dunning] is three up:

> Now all on fire the Chiefs [the players] their orbs pursue,
> With the next stroke the orbs their flight renew;
> Thrice round the green they urge the whizzing ball,
> And thrice three holes to great *Castalio* fall;
> The other six *Pygmalion* bore away,
> And sav'd a while the honours of the day.

Somewhat earlier in the poem, Mathison introduces a man named Bobson, probably a contraction for Robertson, who was a well-known ball maker from St. Andrews, [likely an ancestor of Davie and Allen Robertson], and describes how a feathery ball was made.

> The work of *Bobson*, who, with matchless art,
> Shapes the firm hide, connecting ev'ry part,
> Then in a socket sets the well-stitch'd void,
> And thro' the eyelet drives the downy tide;
> Crowds urging crowds the forceful brogue impels,
> The feathers harden and the leather swells;
> He crams and sweats, yet crams and urges more,
> Till scarce the turgid globe contains its store:

Because ball-making then was so labor intensive, a good ball maker would only make four or five balls a day.

To continue with the match, in the third Canto the two protagonists arrive at the last hole all even, predating the Skipper and the Devil on the 11th Hole by about 150 years. Their drives show that 18th century players faced both familiar and unique hazards. Pygmalion hits too lofted a shot, which is caught in the wind and comes down short. Castalio hits a better shot, but his ball is halted when it strikes a passing sheep and ends up in a natural bunker. Castalio then hits his second shot to about fifteen club lengths from the pin. Pygmalion's [Mathison's] second shot is better.

> A mighty blow *Pygmalion* then lets fall;
> Straight from th' impulsive engine starts the ball
> Answ'ring its master's just design, it hastes,
> And from the hole scarce twice two clubs' length rests.

So now it's up to Castalio.

> Full fifteen clubs' length from the hole he lay,
> A wide cart-road before him cross'd his way;
> The deep-cut tracks th' intrepid Chief defies;
> High o'er the road the ball triumphing flies,
> Lights on the green, and scours into the hole:

Thus, Castalio is down in three. To keep the match going Pygmalion must make his putt. But inevitably the pressure gets to him.

> Down with it [Castalio's holed pitch] sinks depress'd
> *Pygmalion's* soul.
> Seiz'd with surprise, th' affrighted hero stands,
> And feebly tips the ball with trembling hand;
> The creeping ball its want of force complains,
> A grassy tuft the loit'ring orb detains.

The next two lines indicate that even at this early date important golf matches were well attended.

> Surrounding crowds the victor's praise proclaim,
> The echoing shore resounds *Castalio's* name.

And so the first recorded match play "championship" ends with a presentation:

> For him *Pygmalion* must the bowl prepare,
> To him must yield the honours of the war;
> On Fame's triumphant wings his name shall soar
> Till time shall end, or GOFFING be no more.

The bowl Pygmalion prepared for Castalio contained a quart of punch. Let's hope Castalio at least got to keep the bowl as well as drink from it!

About a year after Mathison's poem was first published, the newly formed Honourable Company of Edinburgh Golfers drew up the first complete set of regulations to govern play. These consisted of twelve generic articles (rules) plus a thirteenth specific to Leith links. Among their regulations—individual rules on the order of play, outside interference, water hazards, holing out, making a stroke, and the stroke and distance penalty for the loss of a ball—all remain an integral part of the modern game.

In April 1744, John Rattray, a surgeon, won this first ever open golf tournament and so earned the title "captain of the goff." Rattray, as captain, had the authority to settle disputes between fellow golfers and was responsible for superintending the course in the year of his captaincy. He went on to win the competition two more times, the next year and again in 1751.

William Black, another Scotsman, wrote a much shorter poem on golf that was published in 1792 in a booklet entitled, *A Speech delivered in the Douglas Pantheon on The Pleasures of a Country Life*. About three-quarters of this short manuscript of twenty-four pages is devoted to the speech. The six-page golf poem was "subjoined by the author in order to fill up the blank paper at the end." Ironically, therefore, Mr. Black's golf poem "Game at Golf" has come down through the ages as an add-on. Unfortunately, it includes no memorable lines and is only of interest because of its early date. The title page of Black's work describes him as a "student." His birth and death dates and his relationship to golf remain undiscovered.

One final note as we leave the course and head toward the clubhouse. While doing research for this book and delving into cultures of earlier times, I counted eleven other ways to spell "golf": goff, goffe, golff, golph, golve, gouf, gouff, gouffe, gowf, gowff, and gowffe. Regardless of the spelling, however, and as the stories and poetry confirm, golf has always been both a noble and humbling game for a lifetime.

19th Hole. The Clubhouse

Walking to the "nineteenth tee," we arrive at the clubhouse door, an appropriate place to recite Grantland Rice's "The Duffer's Requiem," a parody of Robert Louis Stevenson's famous "Requiem."

♦ The Duffer's Requiem
(With due apologies to Robert Louis Stevenson)

Under the wide and starry sky
Dig the grave and let me lie;
Gladly I've lived and gladly die
Far from this world of strife.
These be the lines you grave for me—
"Here he lies where he wants to be;
Here he lies by the Nineteenth Tee,
Where he's lied all through his life."

The nineteenth hole is nothing if not a sanctuary for re-hashing the carnage or triumphs of the rounds just played. W. Hastings Webling, a Canadian writer and poet born in 1866, placed poetic voice recorders near the losers and winners of a four ball competition as they conversed at the nineteenth hole.

♦ *After the Foursome*

What the losers said to each other:

So long, Bob	Ta, ta, Jim,
Rotten shame.	I'm to blame.
We couldn't win,	We didn't win
But that's the game.	The bally game.
You played great,	You played fine,
I threw you down.	I was off—
Still, let's smile	You know the way
Though fortune frown.	It is in golf.

What they told the other chaps:

Yes, we lost!	Beat us bad!
Poor old Bob	Jim was off;
Couldn't hit	Might play marbles,
A thing, begob!	Couldn't golf.
Fanned the air	Missed his drives,
Twice at least.	Couldn't putt.
Got my goat—	Lost me "twenty"—
Sloppy beast!	Silly mutt!

What the winners said:

Rather soft?
Right, old thing!
Beat 'em easy,

Quite a string.
Serves 'em right!
Awful rot
Playing with 'em—
Rather, what?

The nineteenth hole has also been associated with "spirit-driven" conversation. However, during Prohibition, from 1920 to 1933, the clubhouses were dry, at least in theory, drinking having been barred by the Volstead Act. A second poem by W. Hastings Webling commemorates this sad state of affairs:

♦ *Departed Spirits*

In a dirge like way, I tune my lay
    And sing of the days gone bye,
The good old times of sparkling wines,
    Of Cocktails, Scotches and Rye,
Of foaming flagons of nut brown ale
    Of juicey J. C's, whato!
My word! How I yearn, for the chance return
    Of those joys of the long ago.

It's a sad, sad thought and my heart is wrought
    With the change in the 19th hole,
Where many a Dub, 'neath fortune's rub
    Has bucked up his downcast soul,
Where many a man who had won his match
    Could tell of his game once more,
And prate of his putts that rimmed the cups
    And ruined a record score.

There are those who say, that we still can play
    Our Golf as we used to do,
And freshen our lips, with sundry sips

From drinks of a bloodless brew;
That we still can sit round the festive board,
And join in the same old fun
With temperance beer, as the cup to cheer,
But we won't—for it can't be done.

The nineteenth hole is a place not only for bending elbows but also for bending the truth. Turning once more to Grantland Rice, we have:

♦ Three Up on Ananias

A group of golfers sat one day
Around the nineteenth hole,
Exchanging lies and alibis
Athwart the flowing bowl.
"Let's give a cup," said one of them,
A sparkle in his eye,
"For him among us who can tell
The most outrageous lie."

"Agreed," they cried, and one by one,
They played way under par,
With yarns of putts and brassey shots
That traveled true and far;
With stories of prodigious swipes—
Of holes they made in one—
Of niblick shots from yawning traps,
As Vardon might have done.

And when they noticed, sitting by,
Apart from all the rest,
A stranger, who had yet to join,
The fabricating test;
"Get in the game," they said to him,
"Come on and shoot your bit."

Whereat the stranger rose and spoke,
    As follows, or to wit:

"Although I've played some holes in one
    And other holes in two;
Although I've often beaten par,
    I kindly beg of you
To let me off—for while I might
    Show proof of well-earned fame,
I never speak about my scores
    Or talk about my game."

They handed him the cup at once,
    Their beaten banners furled;
Inscribing first, below his name,
    "The champion of the world."

[As for the poem's title, Ananias was a biblical figure, who after uttering a falsehood, immediately fell down and died.]

Now, with glasses empty and stories told, it is early evening and time to head home. Had we been at the Bruntsfield Links clubhouse, on our way out the door many years ago, we might have heard remaining club members singing these verses from James Ballantine's "A Golfing Song":

We putt, we drive, we laugh, we chat,
    Our strokes and jokes aye clinking,
We banish all extraneous fat
    And all extraneous thinking.

We'll cure you of your summer cold,
    Or of a winter cough, boys;
We'll make you young, even when you're old
    So come and play at golf, boys.

And between verses, the chorus:

> Three rounds of Bruntsfield Links will chase
>> All murky vapours off, boys;
> And nothing can your sinews brace
>> Like the glorious game of golf, boys.

Thus, the poetry of golf has taken us from the Practice Tee to the course and finally through the Nineteenth Hole. I hope that your time on the *Golf Course of Rhymes* has led you to a feeling of kinship with the golf poets of the past and to an appreciation for their poetry. By transforming their personal and often impassioned golfing insights into verse, these poets of the links have given us a unique way to experience "the glorious game" we all love.

Acknowledgements

Thanks first to the golfing poets of old who made this book possible. It gives me great pleasure to make their poems and verses available to new generations of golfers and readers.

Only the beneficent golf gods could have led me to my editor, Leigh MacKay. How else could I have found the perfect reviewer for this book – a retired English teacher and golf coach. I cannot thank Leigh enough for the interest, care and excellence he brought to his editorial work.

Internet search tools and library sources led me to the old golf poets and their verses. Google was the starting point, but www.worldcat.org, the library resources website, was instrumental in finding the obscure golf poetry books. Also of prime importance was the United States Golf Association's Seagle Electronic Golf Library which contains a few of the books and most of the old golf magazines that I searched page by page.

The inter-library loan program and my Harvard University Special Borrower card, allowed me to thumb through a number of the old books listed by worldcat.org. The following libraries were especially helpful: the Weidner Library at Harvard; the Free Library of Philadelphia; the University of Notre Dame Library and George Rugg, its Curator of Special Collections; the Heterick Memorial Library of Ohio Northern University; the Public Library of Cincinnati; the Minnesota Historical Society; the Wellesley (MA) Free Library; the University of Minnesota Library; the University of California Libraries, the University of Alabama at Birmingham Library; the Mervin Sterne Library and the Lexington (MA) Library. Also, thanks to the Oxford University Library Services and the Library and Archives Canada..

Many thanks to Billy Collins, former poet laureate of the United States, and to Robert Trent Jones, Jr., the eminent golf architect and fine amateur poet, for allowing me to reprint their poems. And thank you to Fran Vaughn, an accomplished poet and my poetry teacher at the Harvard Institute for Learning in Retirement who patiently and expertly introduced me the fundamentals of poetry writing and initially guided my exploration of the general poetry literature.

Others who were helpful in important ways include Dr. David Hamilton, eminent Scottish golf historian, writer and publisher, George Peper, the former editor-in-chief of *Golf Magazine*, Roddy Bloomfield, Editor at Hodder & Stoughton; John Pearson, Editor of the British Golf Collectors Society magazine, *On the Green*; Gillian Kirkwood, keeper of the website www.kirkwoodgolf.com, Robinson Holloway of the Golf Writers Association of America, Suzanne Kreiter, Boston Globe photographer and Brian Siplo, author and expert on the literature of golf.

I also appreciated the warm support of Lorne Rubenstein, Belinda Pokorny, Professor William Johnson, Elaine and Paul Dratch, Regi and George Herzlinger, Nancy and Ed Roberts, and most of all my wife and two sons to whom this book is dedicated.

Finally, because, at least with me, poetry writing must be in the genes, I thank my late father, Philip White, whose poetry has always been an inspiration.

Bibliography

Baxter, John E. and James M. Flagg. *Locker Room Ballads.* New York: Appleton & Co., 1923.

Betjeman, John. *A Few Late Chrysanthemums.* London: John Murray Ltd., 1954.

Bentley, E. C. *Biography for Beginners.* London: T. Werner Laurie, 1905.

—— *More Biography for Beginner.,* London: Methuen, 1929.

—— *Baseless Biography.* London: Constable & Co., 1939.

Boynton, H. W. *The Golfer's Rubaiyat.* Chicago: Herbert S. Stone & Company, 1901 (also, Teddington, England: Wildhern Press, 2008).

Browning, Robert. *A History of Golf.* London: J.M. Dent & Sons, 1955 (The Classics of Golf Edition).

Campbell, Malcolm. *The Scottish Golf Book, Revised Edition.* Edinburgh: Lomond Books, 2001.

Chambers, R. *Gymnastics, Golf, Curling.* London: W& R Chambers, 1886?

—— *Poems on Golf.* Edinburgh: Printed for Private Circulation, 1867.

Clark, Robert, Editor. *Golf: A Royal & Ancient Game.* London: Macmillan, 1893 (Flagstick Books Edition, 2005).

Clarke, George Herbert, Editor. *A Treasury of War Poetry.* Boston and New York: Houghton Mifflin Company, 1917.

Decker, Christopher, Editor. *Edward FitzGerald Rubaiyat of Omar Khayyam.* Charlottesville: University of Virginia Press, 1997

Doyle, Arthur Conan. *Songs of Action.* New York: Doubleday & McClure, 1898.

Duncan, George and Bernard Darwin. *Present Day Golf.* London: Hodder & Stoughton, 1921.

Geddes, Olive M. *A Swing Through Time – Golf in Scotland 1457–1744*. Edinburgh: National Library of Scotland, 2007.

Griffiths, E. M. *With Club and Caddie*. London: Gibbings, 1909.

Guest, Edgar A. *Just Folks*. Chicago: Reilly & Lee, 1917.

—— *The Passing Throng*. Chicago: Reilly & Lee, 1923.

Haig-Muir, Marnie. "Qualified Success? Gender, Sexuality and Women's Golf." *Journal of the Australian Society for Sports History*, Vol. 14, No. 2, 1998, pp. 37 – 52.

Hammerton, J.A., Editor. *Mr. Punch on the Links*. London: The Educational Book Company, Ltd.

——. Editor. *Mr. Punch's Golf Stories*. London: The Educational Book Company, Ltd.

—— and D. L. Ghilchik. *The Rubaiyat of a Golfer*. London: Country Life Limited, 1946.

Hutchinson, Horace G. *Hints on the Game of Golf*. Edinburgh and London: William Blackwood and Sons, 1886 (The Classics of Golf Edition, 1987).

Johnson, Don. *The Sporting Muse*. Jefferson, NC and London: McFarland & Company, 2004.

Keene, Francis Bowler. *Lyrics of the Links: poetry, sentiment and humour of golf*. New York: Appleton & Co., 1923.

Kerr, John, Compiler and Editor. *Golf-Book of East Lothian*. Edinburgh: T. and A. Constable, 1896.

Kerr, John and J. Kenyon Lees. *The Golf Song Book*. Edinburgh: J. Kenyon Lees, Music Publisher, 1903.

Kipling, Rudyard. *Rudyard Kipling's Verse: Inclusive Ed. 1885 – 1918*. Garden City: Doubleday, Page and Company, 1919.

Knight, William Angus. *On the Links; Being Golfing Stories By Various Hands, with Shakespeare on Golf, by a Novice; also Two Rhymes on Golf by Andrew Lang*. Edinburgh: David Douglas, 1889.

Levy, Newman. *Gay But Wistful*. New York: Knopf, 1925.

Looker, Samuel J., Editor. *On The Green*. London: Daniel O'Connor, 1922.

Marsh, Thomas. *Blackheath Golfing Lays*, privately printed for members of the Club, 1873.

Mathison, Thomas. *The Goff, a Heroicomical Poem in Three Cantos*. Edinburgh: printed by J. Cochran, 1743. Second edition: Leith: James Reid, 1763. Third Edition: Edinburgh: Peter Hill, 1793.

Moore, Charles H. *The Rubaiyat of Golfer Guyem*. Milwaukee: J. H. Yewdale & Sons, 1913.

Murdoch, Joseph S. F. *The Library of Golf 1743–1966*. Detroit: Gale Research Company, 1968.

Peck, Samuel M. and Maud Humphrey. *The Golf Girl*. New York: Frederick A. Stokes Company, 1899.

Rice, Grantland and Clare Griggs. *the duffer's handbook of g o l f*. New York: The Macmillan Company, 1926 (The Classics of Golf Edition, 1988).

Rice, Grantland. *Only the Brave and Other Poems*. New York: A. S. Barnes & Co., 1941.

Rice, Wallace and Frances, Editors. *The Little Book of Sports*. Chicago: The Reilly & Britton Co., 1910.

Risk, Robert K. *Songs of the Links*. London: Duckworth and Co., 1919.

Scollard, Clinton. *The Epic of Golf*. Cambridge MA: The Riverside Press, 1923.

Stewart, James Lindsay. Editor. *Golfiana Miscellanea; Being a Collection of Interesting Monographs on the Royal and Ancient Game of Golf*. London: Hamilton, Adams & Co., 1887.

Stewart, T. Ross, Editor. *Lays of the Links; A Score of Parodies*. Edinburgh: David Douglas, 1895.

Stringer, Mabel. *Golfing Reminiscences*. London: Mills & Boon, 1924.

Taylor, Bert Leston. *A Line-o'-Verse or Two*. Chicago: The Reilly & Britton Co., 1911.

——— *A Line o' Golf or Two*. New York: Knopf, 1923.

Thomson, John. *Golfing and other Poems and Songs*. Glasgow: W. Hodge, 1893.

——— (pseudo. Violet Flint). *A Golfing Idyll*. St. Andrews: Wm. Henderson & Son, 1897 (Limited facsimile edition, Cutnall Green, Droitwich: Grant Books, 1978).

Webling, Walter Hastings. *Locker Room Ballads*. Toronto: S. B. Gundy, 1925.

West, Henry Litchfield. *Lyrics of the Links*. New York: The Macmillan Co., 1921.

White, Leon S. "Was Omar Khayyam A Golfer," *Through the Green*, June 2009, pp. 10 – 11.

Wind, Herbert Warren. *The Story of American Golf*. New York: Simon & Schuster, 1956.